Customer
Obsession

Customer Obsession

The secret to creating loyal and brand-obsessed customers for your e-commerce business that shout your name from the rooftops and buy from you over and over again.

By
Kerrie Fitzgerald

Download Your Free Bonus Gift

THE FREE CUSTOMER OBSESSION
BONUS COMPANION COURSE

As a thank you for buying my book, I'm giving you a bonus gift of supplemental information about creating your own customer-obsessed brand, 100% FREE.

Your free gift comes with downloadable worksheets, bonus videos, and resources mentioned in this book but created to help guide you through Customer Obsession.

- 3-Part FREE Customer Obsession Companion Course: Here, I walk you through the key modules from this book, accompanied by videos, cheatsheets, and templates.

- 3-Part Email Sequence Templates: I share my exact email templates to help you nurture your buyers into superfans overnight.

- Additional downloadable worksheets, bonus videos, and resources mentioned in this book.

To grab our complete welcome series workflow email templates that you can plug & play for your business, be sure to download the free companion course that comes with the book- visit the following link to download ***www.kerriefitzgerald.com/cobonus***

Table Of Contents

Introduction

Before we dive into customer obsession and why you need to think about it for your brand, I want to share how I got to know and understand the importance of being obsessed with your customers. This wouldn't make sense unless I shared my story of being an entrepreneur, particularly having a product-based e-commerce business.

After a decade working in corporate marketing, I felt a stirring within me to venture out on my own as an entrepreneur. With a new baby boy in tow and a departure from my previous role in international education sales and marketing, I was eager to embark on a new journey. In March of 2016, I was at the gym, using a strength training leg machine when a sudden idea hit me like a bolt of lightning. Why not start my own business, an online store and e-commerce venture? It was totally unexpected, but within a week, I found myself at a Starbucks in Irvine, California, crafting a business plan and designing a logo. The seed had been planted, and my entrepreneurial spirit had taken flight.

So, in July 2016, I launched a high-end boutique pet brand and online store called The Dapper Dog Box. We sold monthly subscription boxes of high-quality treats, toys, and adorable unique bandanas and bowties for dogs. When I first launched, I had *zero* clue what I was doing, but I knew I would figure it out along the way. I will forever be grateful for that fateful day at a gym when this business idea "randomly" popped into my head and changed my entire life.

As I was developing the brand in early 2016, my intuition told me from the start - *your customers must come first*. That was an ethos I implemented in my brand from day one until the day I sold the business three years later. Customers were #1, and they would always be taken care of.

Over the three years I owned The Dapper Dog Box, this is the kind of impact that results from having the "customer comes first" mentality:

- Thousands of happy paying customers
- Hundreds of five-star glowing reviews across multiple platforms
- Thousands of tagged images on Instagram from happy & obsessed customers
- Customers who happily referred their friends and family to my brand
- Customers who repeatedly made purchases from me, and during the holiday season, I was their first choice when it came to gifting
- A community of loyal customers who loved and felt part of the brand. Instead of just feeling like a customer, they felt like they were part of a family.

I didn't just create a business. I created a solid COMMUNITY of brand-obsessed superfans. In this book, I'll share tactical, step-by-step things you can do to implement this concept in your business. If I can do it, it's 100% possible for you.

As Brands- We Can Do Better

Sadly, most businesses that I purchase from today simply aren't doing much to involve their customers with their brand or even trying to provide a fantastic customer experience. The list of shortcomings continues from boring packaging to lack of engagement and poor or nonexistent customer service.

I've experienced firsthand what can happen to your business when you deeply care about your customers, treat them like humans, and provide an amazing customer experience. You can scale your business without spending a penny on advertising. Let me say that for the people in the back- YOU CAN SCALE YOUR BUSINESS WITHOUT SPENDING MONEY ON ADS. You can also get incredible loyal customers who love your brand, willingly promote you all over their social channels, tell all their friends and family about you and so much more.

If you want your brand to stand out and grow in today's competitive market, we have to create customer-centric driven companies.

Chapter 1:
What is Customer Obsession

I must share a story with you that embodies the true essence of customer obsession. Putting the customer first and living by customer-centric values will create loyal, die-hard superfans. This is the true ripple effect that comes from a brand being obsessed with its customers.

Zach Hilton from South Carolina & His Dog Charlie

One faithful day, I received a dog gift box order from a customer named Zach in South Carolina. A few seconds later, I received an email from Zach asking if we could ship his box out immediately as a special favor. For context, the shipping policy listed on my website stated that all orders would be shipped out within 3-4 business days.

He explained that his beloved dog Charlie was recently diagnosed with terminal cancer, and he had only a few days left to live. He was hoping to get the box so he could do a "bucket list" adventure with Charlie. This included taking photos of him wearing his dapper dog box bow ties and bandanas at the beach and enjoying some yummy treats.

As I wiped away the tears, I knew I had to make this experience memorable for Zach and Charlie. I could have stuck to my shipping policy, but I didn't. There was no way in hell I wouldn't do my little part to make Charlie's last few days special.

I quickly put together the greatest box of goodies I could've imagined. I stuffed that box full of treats and added whatever extra items I could make fit, including a handwritten card, and shipped it out the same day. I felt so touched that this person I had never spoken to ordered MY product for his dog to celebrate his end of life. *How special is that?* He could have easily gone to a local pet store or ordered from a more convenient retailer like Amazon, but he chose my brand.

A week later, I got an email from Zach letting me know how incredibly grateful he was for getting that box out to him and Charlie so quickly. Charlie loved the goodies, and Zach included a photo of Charlie at the beach, wearing a bowtie. Sadly enough, Charlie passed away a few days after receiving the dapper dog box. If the package hadn't been shipped immediately, they would never have received it in time.

I wasn't tempted to stick to my shipping policy because sometimes, you have to break your rules, do what's best for the customer, or do what feels right in your heart.

A few days later, I saw a review on my business's facebook page. You can read it below.

Zach Hilton 💬 recommends The Dapper Dog Box.

"Thank you so much for making Charlie look, feel, and be the most dapper pupper he could be. Charlie had a rough weekend due to the extreme heat and his Leukemia but today was all smiles as he opened his box and was rewarded with gifts. He also said though he may be sick, he still can rock a bow tie with the best of them. We cannot thank you enough for putting a rush on his box and cannot express in words the gratitude we have for be able to make these memories with our sweet pupper."

That was when I realized customer obsession is a two-way street—you as a brand need to be obsessed with your customers, and when you are, your customers will become obsessed with you.

Let's Define Customer Obsession

Customer obsession is not just about providing a good customer experience, but about crafting an extraordinary one that exceeds all expectations. When customers feel a deep emotional attachment to your brand, they become your brand evangelists, spreading the word about your products and promoting your brand with wild enthusiasm.

To succeed as a product business owner, being obsessed with your customers isn't important; it's necessary. By prioritizing your customers, you (the brand) can create a customer experience that is truly off the charts and cultivate a loyal customer base that becomes a driving force behind your ecommerce businesses's success. When you are genuinely obsessed with your customers you:

- Treat them like real humans
- Sometimes break your own rules & policies to take care of them
- Include them in your brand's community
- Create an experience for them that is unlike no other competitor

These things may not seem that important individually, but when you add them all up, it creates a typhoon effect. A surge of love between your brand and your customers. This stuff is the secret sauce to ensure you continue to get sales from this customer, and they literally can't help but shout your brand from the rooftops.

THAT is customer obsession.

Why It Matters For Your Brand

Have you ever ordered from a company, and when you received the package, you felt truly special, like they cared about you? *This is why it matters.*

The company made an effort to make YOU feel good. It's not rocket science, yet so many businesses are completely clueless about this.

You need to focus on your customers for many reasons, but let's look at three main ones.

1. **The future of e-commerce** is skyrocketing. To stand out against all your competition, you need to nail this. If you don't, you will continue to struggle.

2. **The happy customer effect:** When you have happy customers, they buy more, and they spread the word about you. When you create these customer superfans, they do so much for you in return for free—aka, it's like free advertising for you all damn day long.

3. **The cost to acquire a new customer continues to increase**, yet retaining your past customers is 5X cheaper. You always want to get your past customers to buy more. This increases your revenue and decreases your need to run ads to acquire customers.

The Future Of E-commerce

According to Oberlo, "It's estimated that 218.8 million US consumers will shop online in 2023-that's about 65% of the US population shopping online. E-commerce is expanding in every direction and becoming a more integral part of the consumer experience worldwide." 1

What does that mean for you? More and more people are turning online to do their shopping. This means the more shops that open, the more competitors you have, and the harder it is and will be to stand out against them. In order to stand out against competitors and the big box online retailers, you have to not only have a superior product and be a stand-out marketer, but you also have to be obsessed with your customers and creating a stand-out experience for them. By doing that- you will win every time against competitors.

Customers are the LIFE and Backbone of your business. You don't have a business without them, so do yourself a favor and treat them well from day one.

You will become obsolete if you don't make your brand stand out as the e-commerce space booms.

The Happy Customer Effect

When you love on your customers, make them feel heard and seen, part of a community, this is what happens:

1. They buy more products

2. They tell their friends and fam about you

3. They share about you on social platforms

4. They leave you 5-star reviews

5. They remind you of the impact you are making

Let's break this down a bit. These frameworks are the basis for this book, and I want them to sink in.

1. They buy more products from you

Did you know it's a lot cheaper for you to retain your past customers, basically getting them to buy more from you than always trying to get new ones? According to Invesp, attracting a new customer costs five times more than keeping an existing one. 2

While you still need to get new customers, you really want to get your past customers to keep buying more from you. One problem I see from a lot of shop owners is that they get someone to buy from them but then drop the relationship after that. This isn't a "customer" one-night stand, my friends. You gotta get them to come back for more and more.

When they have a good experience and like your product, this becomes a no-brainer for them- but it takes work. You need to provide a great experience, and then after they buy, make them feel special and part of your community. When you do the things I'm sharing here, you will get your customers to buy more and more from you. #WinWin

2. They tell their friends and family about you

Have you ever bought a product and instantly texted your best friend because you loved it so much? We have all done that because we get caught up in excitement and we're eager to share it with someone else.

This exact thing happened to me recently! The Barkday Planner is an adorable pet brand that hosts lavish dog birthday parties for the fancy pup. They launched their online store with a signature "dog birthday brunch gift box," which is a box full of adorable toys, treats, and accessories, all with an adult brunch theme. AKA the cutest thing ever. 3

The second the product launched, I bought a box for my dogs and immediately texted my best friend Nicole, shared all the Barkday Planner's website and social links, and told her she needed this product asap!

That is how this all plays out, my friend. When you create a product that your customers GUSH over, they will tell their friends and family.

3. They share about you on social platforms

This is quite possibly my favorite thing about social media and why you can get free advertising all damn day long when you have a cool product & excellent packaging.

When a customer receives your product in the mail, opens it up, and freaks out because they love it, they have to stop, whip out their phone, take a photo or video, and post it to their feed. Aka, *free advertising.* You want as much of this as humanly possible.

Later in the book, I'll share my #1 strategy in getting customers to take photos/videos of your products and post them to their social media accounts. This resulted in my brand, The Dapper Dog Box, getting hundreds of tagged posts on Instagram each month from happy customers :) That's a lot of free advertising for a scrappy brand that never did ads.

4. They leave you 5-star reviews

Trust is one of the leading decision-making factors when people decide to buy from you on your website. Therefore, if your site lacks trust, you will get fewer sales. Reviews on a website are a super easy way to establish trust, especially for someone who has never purchased from you.

Reviews are also one of the key deciding factors when it comes to purchasing. A review is major social proof and credibility. While you don't need 100% 5-star reviews, you need as many as possible. When people don't know you, they don't know if they can trust you. Reviews help push concerns to the wayside and help them click that "buy" button.

Think of when you want to go to a restaurant or get take-out. What are your steps when choosing a restaurant? You likely open up google maps on your phone, type in the restaurant, and then read all the reviews before you decide on a restaurant. As long as most of the reviews are good, you are on your way to deciding on a restaurant. But what happens when the restaurant has all 3 stars and poor reviews? You likely will not choose that one.

That's the power and importance of reviews and why you must have them on your website, product pages, and external channels like Google, Yelp, and Facebook pages. People read reviews, and if you have lots of good ones, people are more likely to buy from you. On the other hand, if you don't have any reviews, people might X out of the page instead of taking a chance and buying your product.

When your customers are happy, feel taken care of, and love your product, getting them to write a review is much easier. They could write a stellar one that will undoubtedly influence your future sales. Multiple that by hundreds and hundreds—these reviews will have a mega ripple effect on your sales.

5. They remind you of the impact you are making

If your product solves a problem, creates a transformation, or makes someone feel happy, you directly impact someone's life. When you marry that with a brand mission, for example, donating a portion of sales to a charity, you are making mega impact. Once in a while, your customers will let you know how much they appreciate you and love & value your product and brand. They make YOU feel seen and heard, which is a wildly impactful feeling.

Your product likely impacts so many people every day—you just don't know it. Sadly most people who are happy with a product or service, you actually never hear a peep from them. It's the unhappy ones you often hear from. When you get bogged down with customer service problems and issues, it's easy to assume your product sucks or your brand sucks but remember that it doesn't. If you're reading this book, that tells me you CARE about your customers and their experience. You are changing lives daily, my friend, don't forget that.

The Cost To Acquire a Customer Through Advertising Continues to Increase

Listen up my friend, let me tell you some hard facts - **the cost of acquiring new customers through advertising is through the roof** and getting more complicated by the day. You can't rely 100% on ads anymore, it's just not smart, sustainable or setting your business up for long term success. Yes, ads can bring in quick traffic and sales, but only if you know what the heck you're doing. And let's be real, that's not easy because the platforms that host advertising don't make it easy to figure out all the intricate nuances. Plus, running ads can be insanely expensive and eat up your profit margins faster than a grizzly bear gobbling down salmon in Alaska.

If you try to do it on your own, it'll cost you time, money on testing, and most likely won't be done correctly. And if you turn to an agency for help, get ready to drop thousands per month (at the minimum) on their fees, not to mention the ad spend. For a small bootstrapped business, this kind of cash just isn't feasible.

By putting more focus on increasing customer loyalty and getting past customers to buy more, you can boost revenue but also reduce your dependency on using ads to acquire new customers. In today's competitive e-commerce market, keeping customers satisfied and engaged is key to long-term success without relying on paid advertising. So listen to me - find ways to get customers without relying solely on ads. Your bank account will thank you.

Next Steps:

List Out 5 Brands You Love. Write Out All The Reasons You Like Them.

1. _____

2. _____

3. _____

4. _____

5. _____

Make a List of 5 Recent Purchases You Made Online. Who Are They, And How Would You Rate The Experience Of Each One Between 1-10?

1. _____

2. _____

3. _____

4. _____

5. _____

Think About Your Business & How You Treat Your Customers. Where Are Some Areas You Could Improve On?

1. _____

2. _____

3. _____

4. _____

5. _____

Chapter 2:
The Importance of Your First 100 Customers For Your Business

I nearly had a heart attack when I hit the publish button on my online store on July 7th, 2016. I kept obsessively hitting the refresh button as if that would magically make sales appear. I was filled with adrenaline, emotion, and excitement. Nothing is more exciting in the world than the anticipation of starting something new that could "potentially" change your life. The world suddenly feels so big and possible for you.

The best part was I got sales... and not just from my mom or best friend. I got sales from strangers. I remember tears streaming down my face as I opened the customer accounts of the first few people who purchased from me. I was overwhelmed and grateful.

Before I share a story of a special customer with you, I want you to think for a moment. Do you remember the names of your first customers?

Cristy & Kuma, the English Golden Retriever

One of my first customers was Cristy and Kuma from San Diego, California. Kuma was the golden retriever dog, and Cristy the dog mom. When I first launched the online store, I would let customers tell me about their dogs, so I could personalize some toys and treats for them. What's pretty funny here is I still remember Cristy's notes about

Kuma. Here is what she wrote. Mind you, this was from July 2016, and I still remember it like it happened yesterday.

"Kuma is an english cream golden retriever. Super laid back, loves the beach and balls and doesn't have any allergies." She also added Kuma's Instagram handle in the notes, so I followed them immediately.

Since Christy was one of my first orders, I was eager to understand why she bought from me and how she found me. I sent her a quick email, thanked her for purchasing a year-long subscription for her dog Kuma and asked her 1. How she found me, and 2. If she didn't mind sharing why she purchased from me? Christy responded the same day and said that she found me on Instagram and loved that we provided high-quality dog treats and accessories.

In one quick email, I found two insanely important and valuable pieces of information for my business.

1. How Someone Discovered Your Brand & Business

As a new business, this should be your #1 mission. If you know what channels/platforms people discover you on, then you double down on those! This is super important, especially in the early days of your business. When you find traction, do more of that.

2. Why They Bought From You

In addition to understanding how someone found you, it's very important to know why they bought from you. *Remember, there are a ton of competitor shops and Amazon that any customer can buy from on any given day. It's your job to understand why they bought from you.*

The Importance Of Your First 100 Customers For Your Business

Your first twenty, forty, or hundred customers are truly some of the most important for your business. They are the ones who purchased from you before anyone else, and essentially, they validated your business idea for you. They can profoundly impact how your new business continues to grow or pivot. Remember, when you first launch your business, you are NOT MARRIED TO ANYTHING. You will change things, and you will adjust things based on feedback. What your business looks like today is not what it will look like three years from now.

Your first 100 customers will play a key role in that adjustment- embrace it and celebrate it. You can learn so much about your new business from these first customers, so be sure to open those ears wide and listen.

What I find from most e-commerce brands just starting or brands that aren't gaining any traction is that you have zero clue about who your customer is. Without trying to better understand your customers, such as listening to their product feedback, reading their reviews about your products, and getting clear on why they purchased from you and not your competitors, it will be challenging to grow your business.

In order to create a brand that your customers are fucking obsessed with, it's imperative that you actually talk to them. I promise you by having a consistent conversation with your customers, you will learn everything you need to know about your business; what's working, what sucks, and what you could be doing better.

When you can jump into your customer's minds, you will learn everything you need to sell to them easier and get them to buy more from you- #winwin.

To Create Customers Obsessed With Your Brand, You Need To Transport Yourself Inside Their Brains so You Know What Makes Them Tick

When you listen to your customers, you can get a really deep understanding of the following things:

1. WHO is buying your products

2. HOW they found/discovered your business

3. WHY they bought from you

4. WHAT they like about your product or how the product helped them

Who is Buying Your Products

Do you know who your customers are? You may not, and that's OK!

After reading this chapter, you will understand how to get this information better. If you clearly understand who is buying from you, cheers to you, my friend.

You gotta know who buys your products- period. As I grew The Dapper Dog Box, my understanding of my customer changed over the years, but I knew the type of customer I was attracting early on.

- She was a dog mom who cared DEEPLY for her dog. She didn't have kids, so she treated her dog almost like a human child.

- She had a corgi, goldendoodle, or a golden retriever.

- She likely lived in California, Florida, Texas, New York, or Washington state.

- She loves dressing her dog up in accessories like bandanas and bow ties and has no problem dropping $30 on a cute bandana.

- She purchased from me versus competitors because I included the highest quality treats and toys in my store. I also manufactured unique dog bandanas that were super trendy and fun which was important to her.

My products and packaging looked stellar for social media photos. With a beautiful lavender box and products following a theme, every photo would undoubtedly be cute. I was giving them props for content.

The above is a summary of my ideal customer and the people who purchased from me. This evolved over the three years I had the business, but that was the person I was targeting. Once I figured out some of the important characteristics they cared about, I could tailor all my messaging around those things.

When you speak directly to your ideal customer and discard all the FLUFF and vanilla language suited for "everyone," you speak to their soul. They feel like the product or brand was literally created just for them.

Discover How They Found Your Business

When you have a new or struggling business, it is absolutely essential you know how people found you. Was it from Instagram? Was it from a blog? Was it from that podcast feature you had? Was it from a google ad? YOU NEED TO KNOW THIS INFORMATION.

This is important because when you know how people find & discover you, you can do MORE OF THAT! Always do more of what is working.

You might have a small but mighty email list or some followers on Instagram or Facebook, but you want to pinpoint where they came from.

Suppose you know that 90% of orders are coming from Instagram. In that case, that tells you you can continue doubling your Instagram efforts because it converts traffic into paying customers. Being clueless about where customers are coming from is a huge no-no. You have limited time and resources, so you need to understand what marketing channels work for you and bump them up!

Two Key Ways to Figure Out How Customers Discovered Your Business:

1. You ask them

2. Your online store/Google Analytics

1. Ask Them

This is one of the easiest ways, manual but easy. After someone orders, send them a personalized email. (this can also be set up as a post-purchase email sequence in your email marketing software)

Here is a sample script that you could send a brand-new customer.

Subject Line: Hi (Insert first name) How did you find (Insert Brand Name)?

"Hello/Hey/Hi (Insert First Name)

I hope you are doing well. My name is (Insert Your Name). I am the owner of (insert title of the brand). I just wanted to send you a personal thank you message for purchasing my product. As a (small/new/female owned), I appreciate you choosing us over competitors.

As we are growing our brand/ recently launched, it would be super helpful for us to know how you discovered us/ found us? If you wouldn't mind sharing, I would be so appreciative.

I can't wait for you to get your product, please be sure to tag us on (insert Instagram or TikTok handle) so we can reshare with our audience, but I also would love to know what you think of the product.

Thanks so much again."

Sincerely (Insert First Name)

Create a Google document in your Google drive and title it CUS-TOMER DATA. Every time someone replies, drop their name and whatever channel they found you in that list. This way, you will start compiling a list that will provide data. Again to recap, if you see that 70% of people are finding you on Instagram, this tells you INSTA-GRAM IS WORKING, so do more of that. It also tells you that you will need to become active on other channels over time, but keep up the good work and do more of what's working.

Other things you can do to get this information:

Create a survey in Typeform or another platform. You can ask your customers the same thing as above, except now it's compiled in a really nifty little form. That way, you can look at the information as a whole, which can be super helpful.

2. Your online store analytics & Google Analytics

Whatever platform you use for your online store will have analytics that can give you a good idea of where your sales are rolling in from. I'm using Shopify as an example—Head over to Shopify dashboard> analytics> adjust your dates to the last month, quarter, or year, then scroll down to "sales by traffic source."

You will see things that likely say Social, Direct, Search, etc.

Social = social media

Search= they typed something into google search and found you & ordered.

Direct= they typed your URL into their browser.

Google Analytics is a fantastic tool for getting data and insight into how people discovered your brand. Be sure to connect your online store with the latest version of GA and get started. This is a powerful and robust tool that can provide incredibly valuable information.

While these analytics are fantastic, I still want you to email people directly, at least for your first 100 customers. It will provide very specific data that can guide where you should spend your time in your business. This can also spark some great conversations with customers and start building relationships. Remember, we always want to do what Amazon cannot—build personal customer relationships.

Why They Bought From You

When I first launched The Dapper Dog Box in 2016, I have to admit that my messaging was confusing and all over the place. I tried to be the personalized pet box, the organic pet box, the accessory pet box, the highest quality pet box, the supporter of small business pet box, and the box that donated a portion of sales to pet rescues. This sent a TON of conflicting messages to a potential customer landing on my brand-new website for the first time.

So when I launched and started to get sales, I actually had zero clue why people bought from me. Was it because I personalized the items for the dogs? Was it because I donated a portion of sales to pet rescues? Was it because the products I included were super high quality? I had no clue. This is what I want you to avoid.

I realized I needed to figure out why my customers were actually buying from me so I could focus my messaging and website copy on those specific things instead of "assuming I knew" why my customers were buying from me.

After sending countless emails, doing surveys, and having Instagram conversations with many early-stage customers, I discovered customers were buying from me because I personalized the boxes, and we focused on trendy, high-end products. My brand was super bright, colorful, fun, and trendy. People coming my way were attracted to that appeal and the high-quality nature of products and personalized boxes for their dogs.

Overtime, as I continued to scale my brand, pivot my product assortment, and remove the customization piece (because hello -personalized is hard to scale), I found that people were actually most attracted to the unique bandanas we added to the boxes each month. Once I knew that the bandanas were the driver in sales, I revamped everything to hone in my messaging around the dog bandanas and little else. My website copy, images, social media posts, and everything else are much more focused around that one thing because that drives sales and, most importantly, why customers were buying from me.

Always understand why they buy and pivot your messaging to HONE in on that.

LISTEN & Get Feedback

When you don't know why people buy from you, you are doing 2 detrimental things to your business and yourself.

- You don't know how to focus your time and energy on your marketing.

- Your messaging on your website, social posts, and emails will be watered down, vanilla, and won't be targeted. You will have a much harder time selling.

Understanding the WHY behind customers buying from you is hugely important. Especially as a brand-new business, you want to know why they decided to tap that checkout button and pay for your products. The more you can dive into the head and mindset of your customers and know the deep-rooted reasons they buy, the more you can continue to hone in on your messaging that speaks directly to that one ideal customer. This will continue to help you sell more and more.

What Makes These Four Candle Brands Unique

When honing in on our product or brand's unique selling points, you have to be crystal clear what makes YOURS different from competitors. If your product is in a super saturated niche, it's all the more important to determine the key things that make your brand unique & special.

As an example, let's look at candles. Candles are one of the most popular products. They are sold in almost any boutique in person, online, at Homegoods, on Amazon, etc. But how do people choose a specific candle when they have an abundance of choices available?

Well, for starters, it depends on the person. Some consumers will make a purchase based on price first, some will buy based on fragrance, some will buy because the wax is 100% organic and natural, some will buy because of the candle vessel, and some will buy because of the brand's story and how they connected with that.

Many reasons drive consumers to click that buy button, and it's your job to understand why they clicked that button and bought your candle (or product).

These brand differentiators are the exact selling points that make a consumer choose one brand over another.

Candle Brand #1 ***Noura Blanc*** They try to make their candles super unique and one of a kind. They create their candle vessels made of concrete, so other than the wax, the candle is 100% handmade from A-Z. They also choose unique fragrances and nontoxic/clean-burning coconut wax and offer a refill subscription to make the product as eco-friendly as possible.

Their Vibe- Uniqueness & Sustainability

Noura Blanc 1 www.nourablanc.com @nourablancthebrand

Candle Brand #2- *The Fragrant Nest (in Ireland)* They focus on their messaging on their handmade candle vessels. They hand-make their candle vessels and choose unique styles that don't exist anywhere else. They attract people who love to support Irish businesses but who also love unique home decor.

Their Vibe- Unique One-Of-a-Kind Candle in Ireland

The Fragrant Nest 2 www.thefragrantnest.ie @thefragrantnest

Candle Brand #3: *Stroud Simply Southern.* They use an individually hand-carved dough bowl vessel that is unique and can also be used for stunning "farmhouse home decor" statement piece. The bowls are also reusable. They also use a non=toxic wax that is 100% natural and vegan.

Their Vibe- Unique Dough Bowl Candle Holder & Statement Piece for Farmhouse Home Decor

Stroud Simply Southern 3 www.stroudsimplysouthernco.com @stroudsimplysouthern

Candle Brand #4. *Do Good Adventures.* They hand-pour soy wax and clean-burning fragrance oils, making them super safe for your home, kids, and pets. They also donate a portion of sales to organizations focusing on mental health and building self-esteem for children & adolescents.

Their Vibe: Candles That Are Both Good For You and Make The World a Better Place Through Their Donation Initiative

Do Good Adventures 4 www.dogood-adventures.com @do-good_adventures

Each of these candles has unique selling points and brand drivers that would get a customer to choose them over a competitor. It's your job to figure out your brand drivers and why they chose you over competitors.

If you aren't sure what makes your brand special or why someone buys from you over competitors, this is a great starting point for you.

You can use the script mentioned above in "how they found you" and include why they bought from you, and it doesn't hurt to also ask for some feedback :) What did they love the most?

Next Steps:

How They Found You:

1. Craft your email template to ask your first 100 customers how they found you. I gave you the script for the template earlier in this chapter. You can copy and paste and refine with your brand and personality.

2. Create a google doc/sheet and save it as CUSTOMER DATA. Then, every time a customer tells you where they found you, add those details to that doc.

Your Online Store Analytics

1. Spend a few minutes and get familiar with your online store analytics. Specifically, look at SALES BY TRAFFIC SOURCE and play around with the dates. Where did your sales come from? It may surprise you!

2. Connect your online store with Google Analytics.

Why People Buy

What are 5 reasons why people buy from you? Or you can go deeper, list your top 10 products, the main reason for each product, and why people buy.

1. _____

2. _____

3. _____

4. _____

5. _____

6. _____

7. _____

8. _____

9. _____

10. _____

Chapter 3:
Importance of Customer Experience {The One Key Way You Can Be Better Than Amazon}

Last year I ordered a physical planner from the Content Planner. They are a top-rated planner for your online content, loaded with features to keep your content on track and on trend.

After seeing it a few times on Instagram, FOMO kicked in, and I ordered one for myself! After stalking my USPS tracking emails, the box arrived, and I could barely contain my excitement to open it....... it arrived in a brown craft box. Initially, I was disappointed because I expected something much more interesting and fun and less like a plain brown box Amazon style-delivery. When I cracked that brown box open, I was totally blown away. 1

Inside that boring brown box was a beautifully branded white box filled with magic & beauty. There was branded tissue paper and elegant wrapping. It just looked pretty and perfect. It was clear this company took a lot of time to ensure their customers had a stellar experience opening their packages each and every time.

I forgive the Content Planner for using the brown box because what was inside was so special and so scroll-stopping—you nailed it, Content Planner. To this day, this has been one of my all-time unboxing experiences. You can check them and their gorgeous journals out https://www.instagram.com/thecontentplanner/.

Another brand that has totally wowed me with their unboxing experience and packaging is L'atelier Box. I ordered a fancy $80 blanket for myself as a Christmas present. A big box showed up at my doorstep a few days later, and I was blown away! The blanket was the warmest, coziest, and softest big blanket I've ever had, and the packaging was just as gorgeous. 2

The box design is like black marble (so chic, I know)! On the inside of the box, there is a beautiful bold statement, "Hey There, Best Friend" and underneath is a powerful statement talking about how the brand stands to empower female artisans. This gives me all the warm & fuzzy vibes but also instantly humanizes this brand. Instead of receiving just a blanket, I now have a stronger connection & respect for L'atelier Box because their mission is to support female artisans.

That first impression of packaging creates strong, lasting impact in your consumer's mind.

Now that you've gotten your feet wet when it comes to creating a positive experience regarding packaging, let's dive into the full anatomy of a perfect customer experience and how that can look for you.

Creating An Unforgettable Customer Experience Is So Important

Creating an experience for your customer isn't just important; it's imperative. When your customer receives your package in their mailbox or at their doorstep, they should be blown away, wowed, and truly excited to dig in.

When you create an experience for your customer that is so good and memorable, you get them to take pics and post them on their social media (hello, visibility booster), refer friends and family, and buy from you over and over again. Pay attention here. It's that important.

Think About a Recent Purchase You Received In The Mail From A Small Business

(Not from Amazon or a Big Box Retailer)

Did it come in a boring brown box? As a small business and BRAND trying to create customer loyalty, you must do better than a brown cardboard box.

As mentioned above, creating an experience for your customer isn't just important; it's imperative. When your customer receives your package in their mailbox or at their doorstep for the first time, they should be blown away, wowed, and truly so excited to dig into that package. They should also love it so much that they cannot wait to whip out their phone, post videos on their IG stories, and gush over the packaging.

Amazon Versus a Small Brand's Customer Experience

Amazon will always win with fast delivery, free shipping, and ridiculous ease of ordering any item in just a few clicks. But you can win by creating an extraordinary customer experience that Amazon can never beat. 3

Regarding Amazon, the expectations for customers like me or you are two things.

- **Convenience**

  You can literally order just about anything from the convenience of your home, laptop, or cell phone. With just a few clicks, your product is en route to your home. Amazon makes it idiot-proof and easy to order stuff, so you don't have to waste time & energy going out to the store.

- **Free (and fast) shipping**

  Amazon will get most of the products you want to your doorstep in just 2 days and for FREE. Free shipping is one of the HIGHEST incentives for people to click that buy button and buy your products.

Think back for a sec here. Have you ever received a brown box from Amazon and been upset that the packaging is very lackluster? Probably not because you don't order from Amazon to get pretty packaging; you order to get your product delivered ASAP.

Let's Dissect Amazon's Packaging

We all know what the delivered Amazon box looks like, a plain brown kraft box with branded packaging tape to hold the seams together. Inside, the boringness continues with a packing slip and the product you ordered. Their unboxing experience is quite possibly the most BORING thing imaginable.

Before we go on, let's be clear on expectations. You don't order from Amazon to be wowed by fancy branded packaging. You order to get products sent to your doorstep (for free) in 1-2 days. There is less brand loyalty. You just choose the best product that arrives the fastest. It's also important to keep in mind that Amazon operates as a third-party platform, meaning that your purchase isn't necessarily from the actual brand but rather through Amazon as a whole.

Expectations are such a key part of the consumer experience. This is why you MUST think about creating a stronger & memorable experience for your customers so they choose you over the big box retailers.

Next Steps:

Assess Your Product Packaging and Compare to Amazon

What makes your packaging better, more special, and more personalized? Make a list of 5 things you are already doing better with your packaging.

1. _____

2. _____

3. _____

4. _____

5. _____

Dream Boat Packaging

Have you ever been wowed by a box that showed up on your doorstep or mailbox? Was it the gorgeous exterior packaging, or was it something about the presentation of the product? Be sure to also list out what specifically you liked about the packaging. Write down 5 of these below.

1. _____

2. _____

3. _____

4. _____

5. _____

Chapter 4:
How To Create an Unforgettable Customer Experience

K nowing the sheer importance that packaging plays to a consumer's experience, I knew I needed to create something out of this world when it came to my packaging for The Dapper Dog Box.

How I Wow'ed My Customers With Packaging-My Custom Box Packaging Story

Here is a lil secret-I created my packaging design *exclusively for social media.*

It didn't start that way, though. It took me 1+ years in business before I evolved my packaging into a mini work of art. I wanted my customers to be obsessed with it too, but social media was a huge driver of motivation- here is why.

I started with simple packaging when I initially launched my business, The Dapper Dog Box. My products were shipped in a 10X8X4 box, which was kraft color on the inside and a gorgeous lavender color on the outside. It had my adorable dog logo and just a few lines of text. It was cute, basic, and very simple.

This type of packaging is what I would consider "starter packaging." This is when you're early on in your business or not quite making a lot of sales but still want your packaging to look good for your customers.

For me and my business, I knew I would create some epic packaging that would wow my customers and get people to stop the damn scroll when they saw my product.

My first box for my business, The Dapper Dog Box featuring my dog Asha.

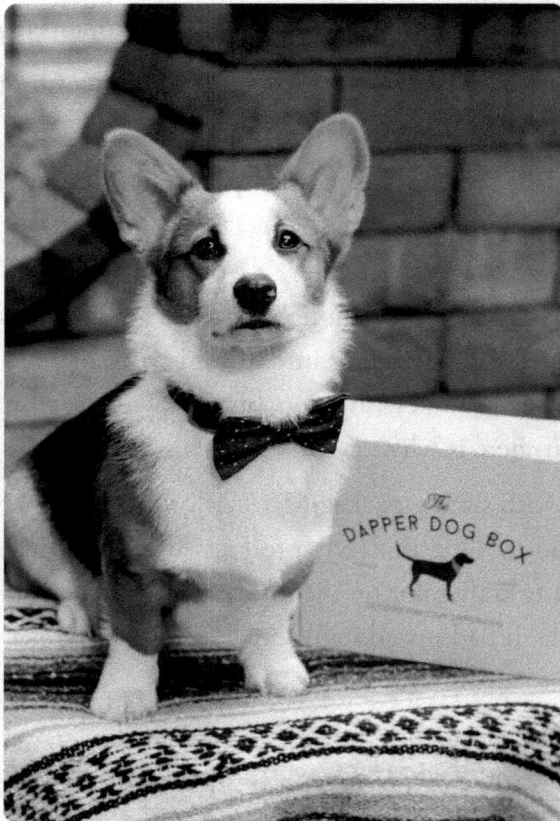

One Year After I Launched My Business: My New & Improved Packaging

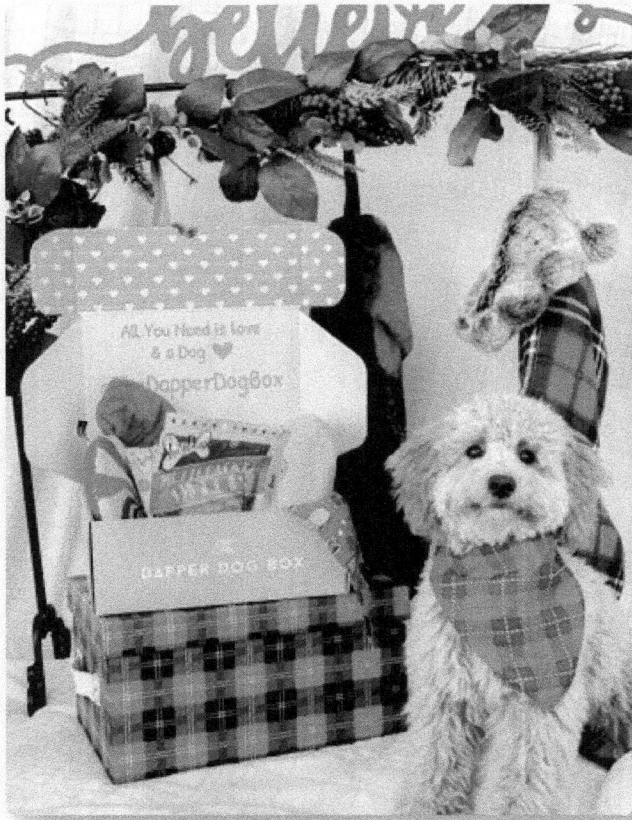

I added interior text to create a magical branded experience. The inside had "All You Need is Love & A Dog" 💜 and then a branded hashtag #thedapperdogbox.

Not only was this a marketing tactic (everytime a customer shared a photo online, my branding was clear & visible), but the box was so beautiful that customers would go crazy to post photos of their box with their dog each month.

Ninja Marketing + Elevated Customer Experience=more sales for my business as a result of the packaging upgrade.

Turning my packaging into something that would cause a frenzy on social media was one of my main goals and intentions when creating it. Vanilla, boring, and plain were all the words I did NOT want my packaging to be.

I wanted packaging that truly stopped people's scroll, so when they came across my product, they would stop and ask themselves- "who the F is this, and how do I buy it." I truly wanted to have the most epic packaging within my niche. I also knew a scrappy logo on a box wouldn't cut it this time. Creating my packaging for The Dapper Dog Box was truly one of the proudest things I did in my business- and still to this day.

To see more images of this gorgeous packaging, head over to my blog post. 1

www.kerriefitzgerald.com/magical-ecommerce-packaging

How I Created Magical Packaging

Creating new packaging designs from scratch seems overwhelming. So let's break it down in a simple way. First things first-I started a Pinterest board and researched packaging designs, subscription box designs, and any CPG brand packaging for inspiration. Since I wanted my packaging to truly pop off the page, I focused on compiling designs with creativity, character, and something that would make my product stand out on social media and blogs.

Anything I found online or on Instagram, I took screenshots. I added them to my Pinterest boards to keep everything in one organized place. I spent months researching and creating the perfect combination of pieces to turn my packaging into a true work of art.

The other thing I wanted to master regarding the packaging was the inside. When people opened the box, the inside would truly wow them as much as the outside. The inside area of your box is prime real estate. The worst thing you can do is leave this space blank. When you have that box opened up, you can utilize that space with your own branding, and you get free advertisement every time someone posts a pic or video on social media.

Box Manufacturer

When I first launched my business, I was getting my boxes printed with a digital printing company in Ohio called Boxup. That served me well until it didn't. The price per box from a digital printing company is crazy!! I was paying $5+ per box for the first year of my business. As my business and subscriber base grew, I knew it was time to level up and look into working with a box manufacturer, using flexo printing. This is a fancier way of printing boxes (we go into detail below), but the price per box drops drastically when you go this route.

A year into my business, I started looking for a manufacturer to work with. I had no clue what I was looking for, but luckily, I found a company in southern California, where I was living at the time (thank you, Google), and we got to work. They helped me choose the color, the right thickness of the box, and everything else. It was a wonderful experience from start to finish, and working with the manufacturer allowed me to get my box pricing down to $1 per box door-to-door.

After months of researching designs, coming up with the best-ever box design, and working with the manufacturer, I finally got my babies delivered to my doorstep by the pallet. They were spectacular. In fact, I'm pretty sure I teared up when he showed me the sample hot off the press. It was pure perfection. All my hard work and research paid off 100%.

I couldn't wait to get these into the hands of my customers. I had a sneaky feeling my business was about to change forever- and it did.

To see more images of this gorgeous packaging, head over to my blog post

www.kerriefitzgerald.com/magical-ecommerce-packaging 1

The Impact

Investing in better packaging had a significant impact on both my sales and the amount of product content that my customers shared on social media, particularly on Instagram. My customers were so obsessed with the new upgraded boxes that they couldn't stop raving about them and expressing their admiration.

After upgrading my packaging, I saw a ***significant overall increase in my sales***. It can be challenging to accurately identify and measure the impact of packaging, but I believe it played a significant role in making my product *stand out from the competition*. For instance, when potential customers are scanning through a blog post listing the top 10 pet bandana brands or human design apparel companies or the top 5 non toxic candles, superior packaging catches their attention, causing them to pause and take notice of your product compared to the sea of others. This is the secret sauce that excellent packaging can provide to any brand or product.

Creating beautiful packaging not only helps sell your products, but also creates an exceptional customer experience. This experience can lead to repeat purchases, word-of-mouth referrals, and user-generated social media content. ***Therefore, prioritizing customer experience needs to be at the forefront of all brands' strategies.***

Customer experience isn't *just* about fancy packaging or how amazing the product looks when it shows up at your doorstep. Customer experience is *the entire process*, from when a customer lands on your website to their getting your shipping notifications, to the package at their doorstep, to the emails after the package is delivered. Unfortunately, most brands screw this up somewhere along the way, so I'm here as your product biz fairy godmother to help you nail this at every stage.

With all the consumer choices people have, creating an impeccable customer experience will keep them coming back to you.

The Anatomy of a *Perfect* Customer Experience, From Website To Post-Purchase Emails

Three key stages make up the customer experience. The ordering stage, the pre-arrival stage, and the product-arrival stage. Each stage has its own unique importance in the customer's experience with your brand.

Ordering Stage

(When a potential customer is on your website/or attempting to order from you)

1. Make It Easy For People To Buy
2. Have a Clear & Simple Checkout Process

1. Make It Easy For People To Buy From You- Period

For the ordering stage, we simply want to ensure your website and checkout process don't discourage people from ordering. Your website needs to be as easy and clean-cut as possible. On a daily basis, I see massive website & web conversion mistakes that prevent you from selling your products easily. Always ask yourself, is my website structured to make it **easy** for people to find the products they need?

Here are some key things you need to make it easy for your shoppers to find what they want & checkout in a simplified way that doesn't deter them from your website.

Menu & Navigation

Are your products clearly displayed by collection in your menu? For example, if you sell skincare products, you would logically label your menu in a way like: Skincare> Cleansers>Oils & Serums > Moisturizers > Masks >Tools.

Do you see how this would make it super easy for people to find an oil cleanser if that's what they were searching for? Don't title collections with funky names that only YOU Know how to decipher. Sometimes I see brands using funky collection names that their customers would have zero clue what they were, making it more challenging to find what they need.

When you make it hard for people to find the products they want, consider that 100% of a sale that you lost. They will be gone and X out of the page so quickly. Your website should be so idiot-proof that a drunk person could figure out how to buy that oil cleanser with just a few clicks.

Here is a great example from Patchwork Pet- a pet toy brand. Their menu has dog toys and cat toys, but a drop-down displays the specific types of toys they sell under dog toys. This makes it super easy for a customer to clearly identify which toy they may want, and then they can click to the right page. 2

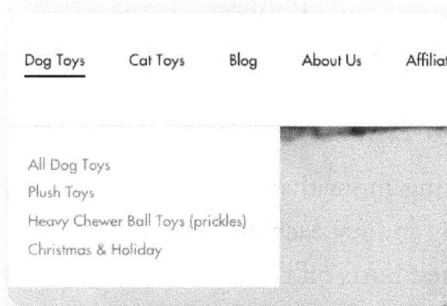

Search Bar

You know when you are on a website, and you can't find what you need, so you search for that little search & circle icon so you can try to search for the product? This is called a search bar; you 100% want to ensure it is enabled on your site.

Nothing is more frustrating than being on a website and being unable to find that specific product you want. You may just forget the product's name or style, and having that search button makes it so much easier to find a product rather than shuffle through hundreds of product pages.

Remember, when you make your customers jump through hoops to find what they're looking for, you've already lost the sale. They're gone.

To enable your search feature, go to your online store theme, and inside the header section, you should see a little "enable search," make sure that's ticked on.

2. Have a Clear & Simple Checkout Process

Is your website checkout working for you or hindering your customers from buying your products? This is where we need multiple payment options and a simplified checkout to seal the deal.

Offering Multiple Payment Options at Checkout

Are you offering more than one payment option at checkout? If not, you are losing money each and every day. People are lazy and do not want to get their butts off the couch to grab a credit card. They also don't want to get off their Peloton bike mid-ride to grab a credit card.

***Paypal*-** This is a given. Like Amazon, Paypal allows lazy people (like myself and 99.9% of people) to buy your product without having to type in their name, address, and credit card details. Hint: When you add Paypal as a payment processor, I guarantee your conversion rate will instantly increase. 3

***Shop Pay, Apple Pay, Amazon Pay*-** Here are a few more that you can add. Shop Pay is pretty much like PayPal. Customers can eliminate the hassle of adding their card details and address with one email!

Reminder, Friend: MAKE IT EASY FOR PEOPLE TO BUY FROM YOU, PERIOD.

Making Customer Accounts "Optional" at Checkout also known as Guest Checkout

This is a really important one. Make sure you do not have "accounts required" on your checkout page. When you have accounts required, you make someone create an account/log in to an existing account anytime they want to buy. This is a big no-no. You will lose people left & right with this kinda behavior. For example if you use Shopify, go into your Shopify settings > checkout > accounts. Be sure to have this toggled to "accounts optional," and you are good.

Pre-Arrival Stage

(This is the stage where someone has purchased a product from you but hasn't received it yet)

During the pre-arrival stage, you want to focus on 2 things:

1. Emails and notifications that welcome them to your brand and get them excited about their order

2. Shipping updates and keeping your customer aware of anything that could make them unhappy when the product arrives- also keeping your customer informed of any delays or shipping issues

This is when most brands just halt any effort, but not you. You ARE different. This isn't the time to say thanks for your money, peace out. This is the time to make your new customer feel like they made the right decision buying from you and make the pre-arrival experience perfect! ***Make Sure They Have An Epic Experience.***

Send The Right Emails

There are a few crucial order notifications and emails you need to set up in your online store/email marketing software. Here, automation IS your friend. Create it once and it's done.

Order Confirmation Email

(This is a notification that you create inside Shopify)

First, this email is NOT your welcome email, which I will share below. You need to have both an order confirmation AND a welcome email. Let's use an order confirmation notification email from a Shopify store as an example.

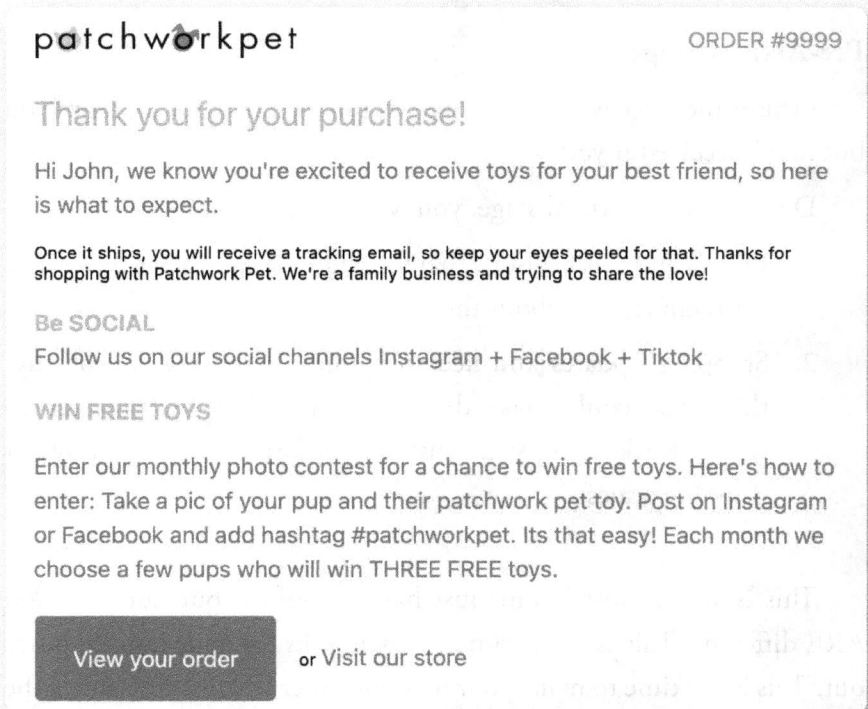

---

patchworkpet   ORDER #9999

Thank you for your purchase!

Hi John, we know you're excited to receive toys for your best friend, so here is what to expect.

Once it ships, you will receive a tracking email, so keep your eyes peeled for that. Thanks for shopping with Patchwork Pet. We're a family business and trying to share the love!

Be SOCIAL
Follow us on our social channels Instagram + Facebook + Tiktok

WIN FREE TOYS

Enter our monthly photo contest for a chance to win free toys. Here's how to enter: Take a pic of your pup and their patchwork pet toy. Post on Instagram or Facebook and add hashtag #patchworkpet. Its that easy! Each month we choose a few pups who will win THREE FREE toys.

[View your order]   or Visit our store

In your order confirmation email, this template is already created in your Shopify account. However, I would head to your account>settings>notifications>order confirmation to see where you can "jazz" this notification up.

Make this branded by adding your logo and brand colors to the button. Make it fun for them, and see where you can infuse a little personality. Nothing is more boring than getting an email from someone you just spent money with and all it says is, "thanks for your order." This email can be simple, but make adjustments and customizations to make it fun or personable where you can.

Welcome Email

(this email should come from your email marketing platform) This is where you want to show your PERSONALITY and truly welcome them to your brand. P.S- this email is one of the highest opened emails you will ever send-statistically, so make it shine.

Tips & How-Tos On Creating An Incredible Welcome Email

Ask yourself- how can I set the tone for my brand new customer so they have the very, very best experience ordering from me that they cannot wait to order again, tell my brand to their friends and family, and feel connected and happy about my brand.

Generally, you would set this email up in the "automation/workflows/sequences" of your email marketing software. These are a series of emails that are sent to a customer based on a trigger. In this case, when someone orders, they are "funneled" into a cycle of emails sent automatically. The first email that should go out is a welcome email.

Four things every welcome email should have:

- **A fun subject line**- something like "Yay, Thank you for your purchase, can't wait to be friends!"

- **A fun image or gif** to set the tone of the email AND your relationship, I would choose a fun lifestyle image that showcases your brand here.

- **A nice welcoming message**. This is where you want to really show your personality. For one of my clients, we have a fun brand, so in the emails, we write things like "Yay, we love you so much," "Whohoho, can't wait to be friends," and show your brand's personality. Are you funny, sassy, serious, or whitty?

- **Make them feel special**. This is where you also want to reinforce their decision to buy from you. You want them to feel like they made a good decision to buy from you.

- **Include key brand/order communicators** like when they can expect the package to be shipped and anything unique or important they need to know about the order/product, ask them to follow you on social media (choose the channel you are most engaged on) and telling them where or how to communicate with you if they have an issue with their order.

To grab our complete welcome series workflow email templates that you can plug & play for your business, be sure to download the free companion course that comes with the book- visit the following link to download *www.kerriefitzgerald.com/cobonus*

Shipping Notifications

Ok, in my opinion, you can't have enough shipping emails. After someone orders from you, the #1 email you will likely receive from them is "when will my package ship?"

Make sure you have your notifications set so your customer receives an email when the shipping label is purchased and when the order is shipped out. These can be set up through your shipping company or your online store like Shopify. You can find this by heading to account>settings>notifications>shipping. Having notifications such as delivered, out for delivery, shipping confirmation is absolutely essential!

Product-Arrival Stage

(the package has been delivered)

Here is where you can really bring the magic to your customer experience. The package has been delivered, now is the time to hopefully wow the sh$t out of them. Remember, we want to be BETTER than Amazon, so I think a boring brown box with a packing slip is NOT acceptable. Your packaging has the true power to delight the hell out of them.

During the product-arrival stage, you want to focus on 2 things:

1. Your exterior packaging and making it impressive

2. Your interior packaging and making your printed inserts/post-cards effective & looking good

Packaging

In my opinion, your packaging is the holy grail of making or breaking a good customer experience. If you want your customers to post endless videos on Insta & Tiktok of your product, do yourself a favor and put effort into your packaging. Your packaging can make a huge impact on your customer's initial experience with your brand.

What Great Packaging Does

Good packaging helps create a great customer experience. Great packaging stops someone in their tracks while fumbling with their phone to take a pic and post it to social media. From a marketing perspective, branded packaging is the ultimate way to differentiate your product from a competitor, create a wildly impressive unboxing experience, and create authentic connections with your customer. Here are a few things that great packaging can do for your brand:

- Creates a customer experience so good your brand becomes etched in that person's brain
- Makes people take pics/unboxings, and videos and post them to their social media
- Gets them to refer you to their friends and family
- Makes you top of mind when they need a gift for something
- Gets the customer to leave positive reviews about you online
- Makes your brand stand out on social media
- Gets people to stop the scroll online

Your packaging matters!

Packaging Options

Now, your packaging totally depends on the products you sell, so whether you want to ship products in a poly mailer bag, a craft box, or a gorgeous branded printed box, the choice is up to you. But let me remind you that you can ***always*** improve your packaging with a few upgrades.

The most common and popular packaging options for e-commerce are poly mailer bags or corrugated/printed mailer boxes. They both come in various shapes, sizes, colors, and thickness, making them super versatile for a wide range of products.

Corrugated Boxes/Mailer Boxes

Traditionally the most popular packaging option because of its durable protection. There are many options when it comes to boxes- do you go the craft brown route, the white route, go for a box with a sticker or packaging tape, or fully printed with a fun design? The choices are absolutely endless, depending on how big or simple you want to go.

We could write a whole book on e-commerce packaging, so let's share a few things to get you started.

Box Colors:

- Kraft-natural brown colored box

- White- white or a variety of light shades perfect for digital or color printing

Box Printing:

- Digital-Digital printing is where a design is essentially "printed directly" on the packaging material- like a desktop printer that prints on a sheet of paper in your home. Perfect for low quantity orders, not permanent and flexible. This is perfect for an early stage e-commerce brand that is still figuring out its brand & customer.

- Direct Printing/Flexography-This is a more complex printing, but think of a huge rubber stamp that transfers the ink in the form of your design and artwork. It uses plates and dye-boards; typically, you will have to go through a box manufacturing company. There is an upfront fee for the plates & boards, so this route is only suitable for brands that are more established and can afford the upfront cost (I paid a few thousand $). The benefit- when you order in high volume, your price per box will be very cheap compared to the higher price point of a digitally printed box.

Digital printing is great for low-quantity box orders and testing out designs and prototypes. Flexo printing is suitable for high-volume orders due to the investment of plates & dye-boards. I have used both options, and both work like a charm.

Poly Mailer Bags

I love poly mailer bags! They are lightweight, yet with some simple branding, stickers, or custom printing, you can completely transform a boring white poly mailer into a gorgeous experience for your customer. This packaging type is super cost-effective, tear-resistant, and waterproof!

Instead of a white poly mailer bag with a sticker, you can go the branded route. Go to stickermule.com and upload a design or a logo. This may sound basic, but you can do a lot with a fun branded poly mailer bag versus a white bag & sticker. 4

If you don't want to make your own poly mailer bags, go and buy some predesigned ones. You can get these at Amazon or other small businesses mentioned below.

Packaging Design

When packaging for your e-commerce business, instead of thinking about what YOU would like, jump into your ideal customer's brain and think about what they love.

Here are some ideas that can not only help you create gorgeous packaging but also an epic scroll-stopping experience for your customer.

If you ship your products in a box

Exterior

- Can you make the box's exterior more fun, personal, or create a super fun design? You can work with a graphic designer to create something spectacular here! Get creative and infuse your brand personality.

- If you want to go simpler, get a fun sticker with your logo printed and slap that on the outside of the box. Even using a printed sticker creates a beautifully branded experience.

- Custom packaging tape can transform a boring Kraft box into something beautiful and branded.

Interior

- The inside of the box is your prime real estate, yet it's generally the part of the box left completely unprinted. Keep in mind the unboxing experience. When customers post photos or videos of your box & product- the inside is what is showing.
- Logos, a brand slogan, a hashtag are all things you can add to the interior of a box to create a beautifully branded experience.
- Refer back to chapter 4 when I talk about my custom packaging story and look at the photos of the interior of the box- it's absolutely gorgeous. You can also check out my blog, where I show the transformation of my packaging for The Dapper Dog Box, *www.kerriefitzgerald.com/magical-ecommerce-packaging.*

If you ship your products in a poly mailer

With e-commerce, you can do a poly mailer bag or a box to ship products.

If you are going the poly mailer route, get creative with your bags. You can use:

- A plain bag with a printed branded sticker. Most people get stickers using their logo.
- A branded bag using a custom design. The custom design can literally be an oversized logo, a logo with a slogan or tagline, or a combination of colors & a logo. You can get so uber creative here.
- A plain bag with just your shipping label. Now you know I'm gonna yell at you if you are doing this option right here. YOU CAN DO BETTER! Even if it's a sticker that will enhance the experience for your customers, remember we are trying to be better than Amazon here.

A plain bag with a sticker is the easiest option. Your bags can be purchased at Uline or Amazon, and stickers can be made at any printing place like vistaprint.com or stickermule.com. For a gorgeous branded bag, my go-to place is a sticker mule. You can't beat the gorgeous bags, and they will knock the socks off your customers.

My best advice here is that once you know your customer, your brand personality and are making enough sales that you feel comfortable splashing out for a custom box design- go for it! It took me over a year with my business, The Dapper Dog Box, to splash out and get a fun custom-designed box, but it was worth it a thousand times over. In the meantime, go with branded packaging tape or a fun sticker.

Start small & steady, but always work to improve your packaging, as it makes a huge impact on your customer experience.

Additional Resources To Help You Create Epic Packaging

99designs.com- you can sign up for a design contest and get lots of options for your design vision, then choose your designer to work with. It's an epic process. 5

Box & Poly Mailer Printing Companies

- EcoEnclose
- Packlane
- Pratt
- Boxup
- Uprinting
- Sticker Mule
- Lumi
- Vistaprint

*References 7-14

Case Study: How She Created
A "Customer First" Brand

Catherine Hildner, Founder of Kitty Meow Boutique (stationary brand) 15

At Kitty Meow Boutique (stationery brand), the customer experience is truly the heart and soul of the brand. To be honest, it wasn't until the shift of "customer first" was made that the business started to truly grow and scale. Making your business about what YOU like & desire in the beginning is great, but that's only going to take you so far. To grow and scale you need to shift your mindset to put what the customer wants before what you want, or what you think they want.

Here are some simple, but heartfelt ways, Kitty Meow has made the customer the heart of the Kitty Meow brand:

We always include a handwritten note with every single order, no matter who is packaging or how busy we get. You'd be surprised how many people are shocked and touched by this simple gesture. When it comes to introducing new product categories we also take time to survey the customer on what they actually want first, before investing in a new product, with a small incentive to get them to take the survey. You would be surprised at what you think people are looking to purchase versus what actually interests them! Every single order is also acknowledged with a "thank you for your business" message, along with a follow up 2 weeks later asking about their experience and encouraging them to leave a 5 star review. These simple touch points keep the relationship nurtured and the conversation going, because at the heart of it, business is truly all about building relationships!

Catherine Hildner is a designer, educator, & speaker with a stationery line called Kitty Meow that is in over 1,100 stores & 13 countries worldwide. Catherine also teaches other brands how to get their products sold in stores too with her Wholesale Intensive and in person event, Ultimate Product Party.

Next Steps:

Evaluate Your Own Customer Experience.

- Are you making it easy for people to buy on your website?

- Are you complicating the checkout process?

- Can you add a better menu/navigation?

- How are your email notifications? How can you add more or improve your existing ones?

- Can you update your shipping notifications

How Can You Improve Your Packaging

Look at your packaging and truly evaluate how you can start improving it. If you use poly_mailer bags/boxes- how can you make them a better-branded experience? If you use boxes to ship, how can you improve them? Make a list and get to it.

1. _____

2. _____

3. _____

4. _____

5. _____

Start A Pinterest Board

Create a secret board inside Pinterest. Search for packaging design or poly mailer bag design and start finding packaging you like to use for inspiration. Once you start looking and finding images you like, add them to your Pinterest board. Once you see how you could improve your packaging, it's time to get to work and make those changes. Make a list of 10 brands with insanely great packaging you found on Pinterest. * If you decide to work with a graphic designer to create your dream packaging, you can share your Pinterest board with them.

1. _____

2. _____

3. _____

4. _____

5. _____

6. _____

7. _____

8. _____

9. _____

10. _____

Chapter 5:
Nail Down Your Customer Service
& Keep Them Happy

It's 2017. I'm enjoying my morning coffee when I see an email that needs immediate attention. It was a pissed-off customer that was very upset regarding her order. She ordered some dog toys, and apparently, her super chewer dog shredded them up in seconds. The customer was ANGRY, said the toys were poor quality, and basically blasted me, saying she would never order again.

Some business owners may struggle with handling an angry customer's email. The initial impulse may be to respond with an equally negative and confrontational reply. However, it's crucial to prioritize the customer- customers are #1.

How I Handle a Pissed Off Customer

I replied to her email, explained that I understood her frustration, validated her concerns, offered to refund her and send her a new toy of her choice. It didn't end there- I also gave her specific recommendations (which I hyperlinked in the email) based on her dog and his chewing type. What happened next, you may be shocked to hear. She thanked me.

She not only thanked me profusely for the incredible customer service, but she actually apologized for her rude email. She said she was insanely impressed with the customer service and would be telling all her friends, and she bought MORE PRODUCTS right after.

THIS is what happens when you treat your customers like actual humans.

I could have:

1. Ignored her email

2. Replied to her email but not give any kind of solution or resolution that put her (the customer and their satisfaction) first

3. Replied with some bland boiler-plate email template response with a no-return policy or something that said: sorry, you are shit out of luck

4. Reply to her email, acknowledge her frustration, AND offer a solution that would make her happy *#winner*

The fourth option is the winning choice here, people. This is my secret sauce, a super easy solution to 99% of pissed-off customer service emails. It's my "Treat Your Customers Like Gold" Framework. It's not enough to make them feel seen and heard. You have to offer a solution that turns the problem around.

Treat Your People Like Gold -The Framework

We've all had customer service horror stories. They are pretty much a right of passage when ordering anything online. Your products arrive late, are damaged, or sometimes don't ever appear. USPS delivers to the wrong house, your neighborhood porch thief steals your package, or you might just receive the wrong product. Another scenario is you get the product in the mail, and it flat out SUCKS, and you want to return it. All of these scenarios warrant some stellar customer service, so pissed off customers can turn into happy customers and not take to Twitter, Instagram, Tiktok, or Facebook to start a smear campaign against you.

Here is what I like to call the "treat your people like gold," framework.

1. **Acknowledge** their frustration and make them feel seen and heard.

2. **Thank them** for being a loyal customer, and let them know you want to make things right.

3. **Offer a solution** that makes them happy.

Like a Burger and a bun, one is not good without the other pieces. You need to do all three of the steps inside the framework to make an impact on your customer.

Acknowledge Their Frustration

I've decided that 99% of all customer service problems can be solved when you simply make someone feel SEEN & HEARD, every last ounce of their bitching, moaning, complaining, and venting. Acknowledging someone's frustration is step 1.

When someone is angry, nine times out of ten, they just want someone on the receiving end to validate their feelings. They are looking for something as sweet and simple as this, "{insert name} I hear what you are saying, and I understand why you are feeling {insert emotion}."

It's literally that simple. Make them feel heard and acknowledge their point of view.

Once you do that, anyone can be 99.9 % times more likely to stop being mad and start being receptive to whatever solution you are about to offer them. In the next section, I will share a few customer service scripts you can copy and format to match your brand voice and start using today.

Thank Them

While making someone feel seen and heard is super duper important, I always believe you want to show them appreciation immediately. Here is the tea, my friend. Every small business or brand should know that every customer in the world{or wherever Amazon is readily used) has Amazon at their fingertips.

People can buy ANYTHING in 30 seconds, with 2 clicks, free shipping, and a product showing up at their doorstep in a few days. No small business can beat that. So by the very nature of you being a small business & brand, you need to be UBER FRIKKEN THANKFUL for any customer you get. They can order from Amazon at any given moment, and you will have no business left.

You need to thank them for being a loyal part of your fam and reassure them you want to make things right.

Offer a Solution

Now that you've acknowledged their frustration and thanked them for being a customer, let's give them the goods. A few solutions that make most pissed-off customers happy:

- Easy return or refund of the product

- Replacement of product

- Both

My motto when it comes to e-commerce customers- just make it right. While there are exceptions to the rule, you can usually appease an angry customer with a return, a credit for a future purchase or a refund. You have the winning combination when you combine a return/credit/refund and a nice friendly email making them feel seen and heard.

The Wrath Of a Pissed-Off Customer

In 2020, a dog chew company called Real Dog got their ass "chewed" out over bad publicity stemming from a single pissed-off customer. A customer fed their dog a turkey wing chew from their November 2020 Real Dog Box. The turkey wing, marketed as 100% digestible, apparently splintered and shattered inside the dog. The dog spent days at the emergency vet, almost died, and left the poor owner with a hefty and unexpected vet bill. 1

Now you can imagine the PR nightmare that can come from a situation like this....... A business has to be very careful with what they say and how they say it, especially when dealing with an injured person or, in this case, a pet.

Unfortunately, in this specific situation, the founder of Real Dog took little responsibility for the incident. Allegedly they told the dog's owner that they would look into changing their wording on the turkey bone packaging and ***to send "hugs" to the dog***.

This feels shocking to you right now, doesn't it? You would think if your product sent someone to the ER & almost killed them, you may offer more than just a little "virtual hug."

The customer is now pissed off because Real Dog brand didn't really do anything to help the situation, make the customer feel supported/ heard, and didn't offer **any** monetary support for her vet bill. When you don't support your customers, they can take things into their own hands, which is exactly what the customer did.

She went to social media, shared her story, and it went viral. She blasted the company for their awful customer service, for not taking any responsibility for what happened to her dog, and simply told her story of what happened.

You may be thinking about some possible solutions real Dog Box could have done to prevent this from happening. I know I was when I heard the story. But instead, Real Dogbox digs themselves further into their grave. They go live on Instagram, bash customers, and call them "poor college students." I know, this story is hard to read. I am still appalled by this whole story.

This blew UP ONLINE, and RDB was deemed "canceled" in 2020.

How Real Dog Box Messed Up

They legit took NO responsibility. They could have easily solved this whole goddamn thing by apologizing to the customer in a sincere way, agreeing to change their product description on the chews, and showing remorse. Had they done any of those things, the customer likely would have never used social media to blast them.

Now, because of the blasting from both parties, if you google "Real Dogbox" you will see Reddit articles and other articles slamming the brand for their poor quality chews and horrific customer service. That shit stays with you like the plague- once you f up and it's online, it can't be undone.

People will not support a company with bad customer service like that, period.

That one incident actually cost them a lot of money in what could have been future sales-(I'm guesstimating here). What happens on the internet is googleable. Now anyone who searches for the brand, Real Dog Box, will see all the articles about them, and this article comes up on page 1 of Google.

https://www.reddit.com › rawpetfood › comments › rea...   ⋮
Real Dog Box, Cancel Culture, Drama : r/rawpetfood - Reddit
I just got an email from **Real Dog Box** about them being cancelled from an incident where a customer gave her 32 pound dog an entire dehydrated turkey wing.
You visited this page on 12/12/22.

The Effects Of Unhappy Customers

Unhappy customers will do more damage than good, so be cautious and aware of what can happen when you don't care for your customers. You literally never know who is on the receiving end of an order. That could be someone with a huge audience, it could be a Youtuber, it could be an influencer, or it could be a mom with a wide reach at her fingertips. Be respectful and be aware that everything you put in writing can last forever.

Bad Reviews

Bad reviews can make or break your business, especially on platforms like Amazon and Etsy, where people will dive head-first into reviews before making a purchase. What do you do when you go to an Amazon site to buy something? You scroll through their reviews. Now a few bad reviews are OK as long as they are sprinkled in a sea of glowing ones. But, when you have all 1 and 2 stars, you must work much harder to get the sale. Bad reviews can destroy your business.

Let's Level up Your Customer Service Efforts

The science behind creating your customer superfan stems from treating them like gold. If you don't have solid customer service initiatives set up, you are missing out on the opportunity to turn a pissed-off customer into a happy one who is raving about your brand to their friends and followers. Don't let the fear of a $10 refund scare you into bad customer service.

By keeping your existing customers happy, they will:

- Buy from you again and again
- Refer friends and family
- Leave positive reviews on your website

These three things turn into MASSIVE SALES FOR YOU.

Here are a few things you can create to make customer service a priority in your business:

- **Create scripts** for a variety of customer service issues you may encounter

- Create a **customer support specific email address**

- **Get A customer support app**, Zendesk, Gorgias, Help Scout, or Freshdesk for customer support

- Have a **clear way for customers to reach you,** and make sure that is plastered on your website

Customer Scripts

Creating scripts ahead of time will save you so much time and energy and make dealing with customer service issues a breeze. Think of a few common issues your customers reach out for help with or complaints your customers make- these are the perfect emails to create a script for. You can create them on a Google doc and dive into it. Remember these are 100% specific to your brand, but here are a few ideas to get you started:

- Customer who wants a shipping update (shipping delay, status)

- Customer who wants a refund or exchange

- Customer who is angry about the quality of the product

- Customer who is angry about the product being damaged upon delivery

- Customer who wants to cancel their subscription

- Customer who has trouble logging into customer account

Here is an example of a s**cript you could create to handle a customer angry about your product's quality.** In this example, I am using my former business, The Dapper Dog Box. Also note I am not keeping the email super formal- I use slang and other abbreviated words that align with my brand personality.

"Dear Susan,

I am so sorry to hear that your dog ripped up the polar bear toy in 4 minutes. I understand your concern and would also feel frustrated by this. You are a valued part of The Dapper Dog Box family, and I want you to be happy with your purchase. I am going to give you a refund for your order and send you a coupon for $10 so you can choose a new toy for your fur baby.

Please go ahead and use code SUSAN for $10 off your purchase. Based on your order and your dog destroying the polar bear toy so quickly, we can def assume he is a heavy chewer dog. We have some amazing toys for dogs like that. In particular, here are my recommendations for your pup. Here is a link for X toy, X toy, X toy. Those are my dog's fave toys, and I can tell you, her favorite pastime is mutilating a dog in seconds and spreading the fluff all over the house-LOL.

Please let me know if you have any questions..

If you do have any questions, you can reply to this email! Have a lovely day, and thanks again for being a part of The Dapper Dog Box family.

Sincerely

Kerrie"

This right here can make a pissed-off customer stop and calm down. They now feel heard and acknowledged, and you offered them a specific solution.

To grab our complete customer service email scripts that you can plug & play for your business, be sure to download the free companion course that comes with the book- visit the following link to download *www.kerriefitzgerald.com/cobonus*

Customer Support Email

Create an email exclusively for customer support issues and emails. This makes it super easy to exclude these emails from the herd of junk that clogs up your inbox. This also makes it easier to outsource these emails to a VA or someone on your team. Ideally, this would be Support@brandname.com or Help@brandname.com.

If you hate dealing with customer service emails, OUTSOURCE It. This is a super important job in your business. Even if you pay someone 2 hours a week to manage customer support, that's one more thing off your plate so you can focus on your secret sauce.

Get Help With A Customer Service App

You can integrate many different apps with your Shopify store to automate and make customer service feel a little bit easier than manually doing it on your own. If your business is relatively small or new, you don't need an application to help, but as your business grows, so will your customer service requests.

With a customer support tool like Zendesk, Gorgias, Help Scout, or Freshdesk, you can manage all your customer service emails in one space, streamline your process, and implement a chat feature so customers get support in real-time. All of these things will help you keep a handle on your customer support issues and keep your people happy. You can get started with Zendesk for as little as $19/per month, Gorgias for $10/per month, Helpdesk for $20/a month, and Freshdesk for $15/per month.

*references 2-5

Make It Easy For Customers To Reach You

One of the most annoying things in the world is when you get a product delivered to your house, you have a problem and can't find the customer service email/phone number. If you don't make it easy for customers to contact you when they have a problem, you will get a plethora of angry emails- that I promise you.

There are a few places you want to ensure clear customer service contact information:

- Create a **contact page** in Shopify or your online store. Be sure to include the ways for customers to get in touch.

- In your **post-purchase email** that goes out when someone orders from you- make sure that has clear ways for customers to be in touch if they have an issue.

- **Inside your packaging**. Make sure to include a note on a printed insert/postcard about how your customers can get in touch if they have a question/problem. This is a great place to remind them of your website, social handles, and a customer service email address.

Next Steps:

Evaluate Your Customer Service and Ways You Can Improve It.

Make a list of the top 5 problems/questions/complaints your customers send you on a weekly basis- these are the things you want to create scripts/solutions for. Can you sign up for something like Zendesk to automate your CS emailing?

1. _____

2. _____

3. _____

4. _____

5. _____

Create Some Customer Service Email Scripts For Your Business. Identify Which Scripts You Can Create Based On Your Business and Common Problems Customers Have

1. _____

2. _____

3. _____

4. _____

5. _____

Chapter 6:

Create Community and Get Your Customers To Be Involved With Your Brand

Ripley & Rue, a female-owned boutique pet brand founded by Jeannie North, is one of my personal favorite businesses to support and buy from.

They started exclusively selling adorable custom dog bandanas, and over the last few years, they have morphed into a vibey badass dog mom apparel brand. Their motto- "we make cute shit for dog people whose dogs are their ride or die." 1

I initially discovered Ripley and Rue during the early days of my own business, The Dapper Dog Box. I was hosting a dog bandana brand search to find new makers to partner with and essentially hire to make the bandanas we sold in our online store & subscription box. A friend recommended Ripley & Rue, and we connected over Instagram and quickly became business friends. Over the years, I have seen Jeannie and her incredible brand grow to some unreal levels, and personally, it's been so rewarding seeing another female founder grow a brand on their own terms.

One of the things Jeanie & Ripley & Rue have done so well is create a sense of community for their brand and customers. **Here's how:**

Customer Images & UGC Content

Ripley and Rue's Instagram feed is fluttered with an abundance of customer images. The brand takes all the adorable user-generated content (UGC) submitted by its customers and creates a visually stunning, relatable, and engaging dog mom community on Instagram. The images and videos are highly entertaining, and by regularly featuring her customers' content, Jeannie fosters a sense of belonging and loyalty among her customers. This approach enables them to feel connected and invested in the Ripley & Rue brand.

Content That Sparks Conversations

She has a deep understanding of her customer base and their interests, and leverages this knowledge to start conversations that drive engagement on Instagram.

One of her notable strategies is creating content that resonates with her target audience, such as posts on Instagram that humorously proclaim the superiority of dogs over humans. These bold statements spark enthusiastic conversations and debates in the comments section, creating a sense of community and a loyal following around her brand.

By using this approach, Jeannie has cultivated a social media presence that effectively captures the attention of her ideal customer and prompts them to engage with her brand.

With every post that speaks to their interests and values, Jeannie continues to deepen her connection with her audience and grow Ripley & Rue's reach.

These two things create a massive sense of community on her Instagram. Her customers feel like they know R&R. They feel connected to the brand and are likely mega supporters of the brand. She draws people in to have real conversations. This makes people feel seen, heard, and part of something- that is the secret sauce. Whatever you can do to make your customers feel part of your brand- you will win.

Why You Need To Involve Your Customers & Create a Community Around Your Brand

Allie Ruby, the founder of sweary apparel brand *Pseudo Force*, is one of the incredibly talented female-owned brands inside of my signature program, The Cultish Product. It's no wonder she has built a loyal group of customers who cannot get enough of her products. 2

"I pretend my followers + customers are my best friends. Every story, reel, TikTok, YouTube, and email I think 'I'm making this for my bestie'. The message is heard + I build on that relationship by replying to every DM, comment, and email. I've built so much trust and love from customers! People are always telling me they have reminders and alarms set for drops. They say they will never miss a drop."

-Allie- Pseudo Force

Take a moment and reflect on the amount of effort and time you spend on getting every sale. You are posting on Instagram, making Tiktok videos, sending emails, creating blogs, and doing all the shit. You're on an endless content creation hamster wheel that you can't seem to escape- it's exhausting!

Wouldn't it be nice to get that same customer who bought from you the first time to buy from you again and again? Wouldn't your life be so much easier if we removed all the stress from constantly getting new customers for your business?

Getting repeat business over and over again is exactly what you can expect when you "invite" that customer to be part of your brand and not ditch them the second they whip out their credit card and buy from you. This happens because you draw them in and make them feel connected to your brand, making them feel special in return.

When you make your customers feel special & connected to your brand, you can expect this:

- You get them to do things for your brand, such as referring friends and family, posting incredibly glowing product reviews, buying more of your products, and becoming their go-to for gift-giving.

- They create content for you (videos and images) and plaster it all over their Instagram or TikTok. HELLO, FREE advertising for you.

ALL of this above is free advertising, more visibility, and money in your bank. You need this and should always want these things from your customers. Ideally, you want them to keep buying from you, continue the wonderful cycle of them buying, talk about you on social media, tell friends and family, share photos, and so much more.

I want you to take a moment to think about some of your recent online purchases from small businesses

After you ordered, did you ever hear from them again? Did you get some emails in the days and weeks following your order that made you feel appreciated, seen, and heard? Did you get an email where you learned a bit more about the brand?

Did you post an unboxing video or image of your product and tag them on Instagram/Tiktok? Did they reply to your post? Did they send a DM on Instagram to say thank you? Did they reshare your video or post it on their feed?

If the answer to most of these is NO, how on earth would you expect that customer to feel any connection or pull towards that brand or want to buy from you again? They end up feeling like an ATM or, even worse, a purchase from a faceless brand they have zero connection with.

In reality, 90% of brands do NOTHING after customers order from them. It happens to me all the time, and it saddens me because these brands will never grow to their full potential if they don't involve their customers after purchasing. This chapter is dedicated to the amazingness that involving your customers will do for your brand and bank account.

You want to turn your customer into a superfan obsessed with your brand. So stop sending products to your customer and then ditching them/ignoring them until you have your next sale.

How To Create Genuine Connections With Customers After They Buy

Create A Sense of Community Through Social Media

I used Instagram to create a massive community for my brand, The Dapper Dog Box- 42,000 Instagram followers and a tight-knit community of customer superfans later. Throughout this chapter, I share specific strategies that I implemented to grow my account with followers and turn them into loyal customers.

Social Media

Love it or hate it, social media is the single-handedly easiest way to connect with your customers after they buy. Stop complaining about Instagram's algorithm or Tiktok's trendy videos and put in the effort here- it will pay off.

Here are a few ways to make your people feel special when they post about your product on their Instagram.

1. **Comment on the post** - say thanks or leave a thoughtful comment about how grateful you are they are part of your fam.

2. **Get in the DM's**-Send a DM and say thank you! Instagram allows you to literally chat with your customers, don't think of this as a chore but rather a frikken privilege.

3. **Reuse their content**-Reach out to get permission, then reuse that image or video or reel for your own feed- hello, free user-generated content.

This is such an easy one, and I see so many brands doing NOTH-ING when their customers are making a huge effort to promote YOUR brand

Social Media-Commenting On The Posts

When customers take the effort to take photos and videos of your products and splash them all over their social media- you need to comment!

This may feel overwhelming, tedious, or something you think isn't important, but it's super important- and a little goes on a long way!

When it comes to social media, it cannot be a one-way street. You know that relationship where you are dropping comments, replying to story videos, and you hear crickets on the other end? That gets old fast, and after a few times of you making an effort and hearing crickets- you will stop making an effort. This is commandment #1 of social media. You have to keep it a two-way street of communication.

10 Minute A Day Instagram Strategy

Here is a foolproof, easy enough way to keep up with your comments on Instagram & Tiktok to keep your audience & customers engaged and coming back for more.

Spend 10 minutes each day in the morning and dedicate that exclusively to replying to comments. If you start aimlessly scrolling, 45 minutes will pass, and you will wonder why you're still watching Emily

Mariko's cooking videos. Dedicate this time to commenting only! I like to start with my notifications and reply to those first, and then I like to go through the last week or so of posts and scroll through the comments to see if any new ones have popped up. 3

After reviewing my post comments, I move on to tagged images. These are images or videos that people have tagged me in. I look for customer/ UGC content with my product and show my LOVE to those posts. This can be in the form of thanking them for the post, thanking them for supporting your business, etc. I like to make these posts a big deal because this customer took the time to take a photo/ video of your product—show them love, my friend. I also like to save these posts (on Instagram) into a "saved" image folder to keep track of my customers and the content they created for me. Oftentimes I will go through those images at a later date and DM them, asking for permission to use their image on social, email, or on my website.

Scrappy Instagram DM Strategy

Whenever a customer tags me in an image or video, I make it a point to send them a DM. This really supercharges the relationship and humanizes YOUR brand because - does Amazon DM you to say thanks for buying? Well, you know the answer to that. Here is my super scrappy Instagram DM strategy that creates major customer loyalty in a mere few seconds.

I send them a copy & paste-style message in the DM's that can be personalized. I use the notepad feature on my iPhone and quickly copy and paste into Instagram Dm, OR you can create a saved response inside Instagram (google how to do this) it will change your whole perspective on Instagram DMing.

I thank them for being a loyal part of my brand/make sure they feel I appreciate them as a customer. This is a typical message I will send someone on Instagram.

"Hey (Insert Name)

Thank you so very much for sharing a photo/video of (insert product). I really appreciate you taking the time for our brand! Would you mind if we used this photo in our marketing, like website, email, or social? We will be sure to give you credit. Thank you so much again. We are so grateful for amazing people like you. Here is a coupon for 15% off your next order as a Thank you for all the love!"

- Kerrie

You can customize this script to your liking, but the point here is that you are getting your customer to communicate with you on a super intimate channel!

Resharing Their Content

When your customers tag you on Instagram with a photo or video they took of your product or of using it, you want to share it on your feed. This not only makes them feel super special, but you now have free content that can spice up your bland Instagram feed. The more images of customers you share, the more OTHER customers will take photos of your products in the hopes of getting features on your account. You can also use their images for your own content!

Sharing your amazing customer images/videos should be one of your MAIN content forms for Instagram or Tiktok. These video clips or images can be posted on your Instagram feed, reels or posts, Instagram stories, and TikTok videos.

This type of content is called UGC (user-generated content) and is amazing for various reasons:

1. It's content you don't have to create, yet it is available instantly for your Instagram or TikTok without doing any work. #winwin

2. This makes your customers feel special and happy because you've taken the time to share their video/image, and you are, in turn, showing them some love. As a result, they feel appreciated and likely super excited.

3. People trust UGC-type content 10000% times more than anything YOU, the brand, would create. This content is authentic and trustworthy. It will help other people make a purchasing decision because they see a normal regular person using the product.

This effort takes seconds, but it builds relationships with your customers, and they WILL remember you because you will be that one brand that took the time to say thank you, make them feel appreciated, and reposting their content is the icing on the cake!

Engage With Your Customers

Now that you know how to make your customers feel connected to your brand by commenting on their posts, it's time to take it up one notch and engage a bit. This part is the "secret" sauce of building community. You are taking it one step further in relationship building. Once you establish a customer from your brand, you want to engage with them.

Allocate 10 minutes a day- that's it. This is where you, a VA, or your team engages with your customers daily. You drop thoughtful comments on posts or reply to stories. When you are a small brand, you will get to know your loyal customers on Instagram. You see their constant tags and story tags, so you take notice.

Replying to comments, sending DM's, etc., keeps the conversation a two-way street, and it's essential to growing a community on social media, especially when you are a small fish in a big pond. Customers instantly feel more connected to your brand because you took that little time and made an effort for them. It's such a win-win.

Create A Sense of Community Through Email Marketing

After a customer buys from you, part of your overall email marketing strategy is to leverage email to connect them to your brand and encourage them to do things for your brand. You can do this through some basic email automation that ask them to follow you on social media, take photos or videos of your product and post on their social media channel of choice, inviting them to join a customer referral program if you have one or even buying other best selling products they may love in addition to the one they already purchased.

Unfortunately, many brands I buy from do not email me after purchasing. This is such a missed opportunity, but this can hopefully encourage you to prioritize email marketing in your business. The best part is that most of this can be set up once and automated.

Set Up Email Automation

Inside your email marketing platform, you can create a series of "workflows" or "email automations." These emails are created once and then automatically sent based on triggers. In this situation, the trigger is when someone purchases a product from you.

Post Purchase Email Sequence

Here is an example of the emails you could put in your post-purchase sequence.

- Email #1: You are welcoming them to your business family and sharing a bit about why you started the company/why it's important to you!

- Email #2: Follow you on social media

- Email #3: Any specific things you need to know about the product/order/ common questions/ problems that occur with the product

- Email # 4: Push people to post videos/photos of product unboxing on social media

- Email 5: Encourage them to leave a review or share a testimonial

- Email 6: Get them to refer a friend or family member/join a referral/rewards program

- Email 7: Optional - discount code for future purchase

**To grab our complete post purchase series workflow email templates that you can plug & play for your business, be sure to download the free companion course that comes with the book- visit the following link to download *www.kerriefitzgerald.com/cobonus*

The purpose of these emails is they invite your customer to *feel* part of your brand. If you don't ask them to join your rewards program, they won't. If you don't ask them to leave a review, they won't. If you don't ask them for images & video clips, they may not send them to you.

You need to invite your customers to be part of the journey with you. When you do this, they feel more connected to your brand, and your brand is more top of mind to them. They talk about you more, post about you more, tell their friends and family about you more, and buy more from you.

Next Steps:

Do You Involve Your Customers After The Sale?

Take some time and think about how you can improve this critical step in your business.

- Do you have a process for engaging with your customers on social media? Are you taking time each day to comment on their posts, replying to DM's, or resharing their content?

- Tip- Create a 10-minute event in your calendar that recurs each day and spend those 10 minutes engaging, commenting, and resharing customer content on Instagram. When it's in your calendar, you won't forget

- Do you have a post-purchase email automation created? If so- how can you improve it? If you don't have one, now you can create it. Remember, your post-purchase emails are there to do the work for you.

Chapter 7:
Customer Retention & Loyalty-Get Them To Come Back For More

Customer retention begins with one purchase, so you have one shot at making that experience for your customer so great, that they have ZERO choice but to come back for more, and your brand becomes top of mind. According to an article from Motista, featured in PRnewswire, a customer who has an emotional connection to a brand will likely spend twice as much and have a 306% higher customer lifetime value. 1

This means you need to focus more on creating that solid connection to your brand, which creates that special "like know & trust," and in the end, gets them to support you even more.

The $100 Hot Sauce

Here is a story of how one hot sauce subscription box for $100 turned into thousands of dollars in repeat sales for a brand.

Last year I purchased a hot sauce subscription box from Fuego Box. As someone virtually obsessed with hot sauce, this product couldn't get to my door any quicker. It was a 3 month subscription where you received 3 bottles of small-batch hot sauce each month.

Upon receiving my first order, I was blown away by the overall experience. The three bottles of hot sauce, along with the charming packaging, informative inserts on ideal food pairings, and regular shipping updates, left a lasting impression on me. 2

Fast forward to a few months later, when I was thinking of a gift idea for a friend. Guess which brand came to mind? Yup, the hot sauce brand. I loved it so much that they came to mind when I needed a gift idea. I bought it as a gift for a friend's birthday, and then I bought a 6-month subscription for my godson for his birthday gift, then as a gift for my husband. Since first discovering the hot sauce brand, I have spent over $2000 with them.

.......But it all started with that first purchase of a 3-month subscription for $100. That one purchase turned me into a customer superfan, and the brand didn't have to do any extra marketing or anything special to get me to buy more products from them.

This is the dream for brands just like you. You get a customer for the first time, and then they continue to buy from you over and over.

Had my initial purchase been anything less than impressive - whether due to poor product quality, shipping issues, or a lackluster packaging and customer experience - I would not have considered buying from them again. Therefore, creating a remarkable first-time experience for customers is key. Once you've *hooked them in*, you've captured their loyalty. You become the go-to brand for their gift-giving needs or future product purchases, cementing a long-term relationship between customer and brand.

Customer Retention- What It is & Why You Need It

How would it feel if you could get customers that purchased from you in the past to come back over and over again with almost zero effort on your end that it feels almost like "sales on auto-pilot?" That's the dream, right? This is a possibility and should be part of your customer acquisition strategy. Let's dissect this a bit so you understand why retaining your customers is the way to go.

First-what is customer retention?

In the most basic nutshell, customer retention rate is the number or percentage of people who make repeat purchases from your online store. For example, If you sell to 1,000 people each month and 250 people return to make another purchase at some point in the next year, your customer retention rate would be 25%. In a perfect e-commerce world, your customer retention rate continues to increase, meaning you are getting many repeat customers, costing you $0 to acquire.

Here is a sobering AF statement that will get you to hopefully understand the importance of getting your past customers to buy more from you. According to Invesp, It costs five times as much to attract a new customer than it does to keep an existing one. 3

It's always cheaper for you to keep your customers happy and get them to buy more from you, as opposed to always searching and trying to get new customers- just like I shared above with the hot sauce example. It truly can feel like the easiest $$ you make in your business.

Let's talk about running ads and the cost of acquiring a new customer using advertising to grow your business. You may have read about the glory days of running FB & Instagram ads and being able to get new customers for pennies. Sadly, that doesn't exist anymore. Since Apple rolled out new privacy laws against companies like Facebook and Instagram being able to track you, now it's harder and more expensive than ever to run ads. You might run an ad with a $4.99, $10.99 customer acquisition cost or even higher. With ios privacy updates, the cost to acquire a first-time customer has skyrocketed over the last few years. 4

According to Shopify, "As iOS 14 rolled out and paid acquisition became a highly competitive space, investors are looking at CAC to

LTV ratios, and businesses are learning that retention is not just about squeezing more money from current companies, but rather a somewhat direct route to creating brand evangelists and superfans." 5

As a marketer and someone who created a multi 6 figure revenue-generating business without using ads and relied on getting customers to buy over and over - it's so important to me that brands like you know & understand how to get a paying customer without relying on advertising.

This book is all about using customer loyalty as a means to attract and retain customers instead of relying solely on advertising. It aims to guide you in creating a business that can generate sales effortlessly, where customers become enthusiastic about your brand and make repeat purchases, endorse your business on their platforms, and think of you first when they need your product.

The more effort you can put into creating a stellar experience for your customers, your brand & shop will continue to be top of mind when they need a gift or a refill of whatever your product is.

Customer retention comes from a culmination of many things. It's a 360-degree experience. It starts with your website and making it easy for people to buy, following through on any promises your website or product pages promised (like shipping the product out in 2 business days, for example), and sending them shipping updates to keep them informed, replying to any customer service type emails promptly and of course, having nice or beautiful packaging, and a great product so when they open that package from the mailbox- they are beyond wildly impressed.

All of these different pieces play a part in the customer's experience with your product. This determines if they will buy from you again. THIS is why I stress the importance of customer experience. If you sell a $50 product and someone buys it, that $50 purchase could easily result in $500 in sales, $1000 in sales, or more, all without ANY EXTRA work because you worked at the front-end to retain a customer.

Retention Stats You Need To Know

Key metrics to benchmark your e-commerce customer retention include:

- **Customer lifetime value (CLV):** If the average customer makes three purchases of $40 each, your CLV would be $120. Use this to measure the effectiveness of the retention strategy. 5

- **Customer or revenue churn:** The percentage of customers who leave a business over any given period. This is particularly helpful if you have a subscription box or subscription-based product. 6

- **Customer loyalty rate:** The percentage of existing customers who join your loyalty program.

According to Val Geisler, customer advocacy lead at Klaviyo, "Retention is about revenue. Sure, you could think about acquisition when you think about revenue. 'How do we bring more customers in to combat the customers we're losing?' And you're right. That's a piece of the puzzle. But if you only focus on getting new customers, giving little thought to the ones you've already attracted, you're missing a giant piece of the puzzle. More DTC brands could benefit from putting as much focus on retention as they do on new customer acquisition." 7

Steps To Retain Your Customers

This book is dedicated to helping you retain your customers and turn them into massive brand evangelists and superfans. Let's summarize a few key areas we've covered in this book and then dive into a few additional tactics you can implement.

- Listening To Your Customers (chapter 2)

- Customer Service (chapter 5)

- Improving Your Customer Experience (chapter 3)

- Create Community (chapter 6)

You have to nail all of the above things, but let's dive into some additional strategies you can add to your shop to make retention and customer loyalty easier.

Email Marketing

This one is the elephant in the room, my friends. Email marketing is one of the easiest ways to get customers to come back and buy more. In addition to your post-purchase emails we discussed in Chapter 6, let's talk about a few ways you can incorporate email marketing.

- Send consistent emails promoting new products or collections

- Send emails to past customers and offer a coupon code to buy another product

- Frequently promote your products as gifts for specific holidays like Christmas, Hanukkah, Mother's Day, Father's Day, etc.

- Be consistent with email marketing in general. Aim for sending at least one email per week to your list- for example, nurturing emails (sharing content, blog posts, repurposed posts from social media) and sales-driven posts promoting products and sales.

Loyalty & Customer Referral Programs

As you build up your customer base, customer loyalty programs are one of the smartest things you can incorporate into your customer retention strategy. According to Shopify, "A loyalty program creates impactful customer experiences that keep shoppers coming back, even through economic uncertainty." 8

Truth- it's harder than ever to become top of mind to a customer. There are just SO many choices. But I know with what I shared in this book, you can truly become top of mind to your customers!

With that said, customer loyalty & rewards programs are a stellar & easy way to get your customers to buy YOUR product versus your competitors. A customer loyalty program motivates and entices your customers to buy more frequently from you, increases their AOV (average order value), and drives additional engagement to your brand. Typically a loyalty program gives customers points towards a free product or points they can use towards a future purchase. According to Forbes, consumers who are already enthusiastic about a brand are more likely to continue buying and are a prime market for that brand's new products. 9

Customers who come back and buy from you are crucial. These truly are your brand VIP's. As we talk about so much in this book, your customer superfans are the ones who will not only keep buying from you but will be the ones gushing over your products to their friends and sharing it with the world on their social media platforms. When you combine this and offer an incentivizing loyalty program, you will WIN at your business because you aren't always having to chase the next sale. Instead, they come to you passively.

Make Your Loyalty Program Effective

For a loyalty program to work effectively, there needs to be a few key things it has.

- It needs to be **enticing to the customer**
- It needs to be **easy to access** and easy to navigate
- It needs to be **easy to redeem** the points/rewards

Enticing the customer

Sometimes loyalty programs make it too hard for the customer to actually accumulate enough points to get a reward or a free item. You absolutely want to make sure your points + reward system is fair enough that it entices that person to buy more and not give up because they don't think they will ever rack up enough points to make their time & money worth it.

Easy To Access

Once you set up a program (more on this in the next chapter) it needs to be relatively easy enough to find & discover and sign up. Most popular customer loyalty apps will have an easy onboarding process/application process for the customer, so don't worry too much about this. The other thing you need to do is make it glaringly obvious that you OFFER a loyalty program. The problem won't likely be your program; rather it will be that your customers don't know it exists.

You can add a note about your customer loyalty program to your post-purchase email sequences, which we talked about in Chapter 6. You can add this to your website menu/navigation & footer. You can create a page on your website that tells your audience about your loyalty program. When you make it easy for people to find it, they will sign up.

Easy To Redeem Points

Once your customers are buying more and getting more points, you need to make it easy for them to redeem them. A typical loyalty app will use coupon codes and award the customer with a coupon code once they reach a certain amount of points. This will always depend on your chosen loyalty app, but typically, this is the standard format. It's easy, and it works.

Loyalty Programs Make Your Customers HAPPY. As if there wasn't a more important reason to offer a loyalty program- it makes your people happy! When people get things for free, they want to return for more.

Customer Loyalty Program Options

Now that you understand all about loyalty programs and how to set them up and incentivize your people, I want to share a few easy apps you can connect to your Shopify store to set this up in a breeze. There are a bunch of options you can go for, from paid apps you can connect your Shopify store to, all the way to DIY options.

Loyalty Apps That Connect With Your Shopify Store:

- Smile * this is my recommended one
- Yotpo
- Referral Candy

*references 10-12

In terms of which one you choose- look at the options and look at what's important for you and your customers. The majority of these apps will offer things like discounts towards a future purchase, free shipping, etc. This concept is something that smaller brands need to start incorporating- online stores or brick & mortar.

My personal favorite is Smile. It's easy and simple to set up- you can literally connect this to your Shopify store in 20 minutes or less. They have solid rewards options for your customers, and it's easy for them to sign up, navigate, and access points.

Loyalty Program Case Studies

Case Study: Primally Pure

Primally Pure is my favorite brand when it comes to skincare products, and I am a loyal superfan customer who is obsessed with their products. One of the reasons for my loyalty is their exceptional rewards program, which encourages me to purchase more of their products by offering rewards for every dollar I spend. When I join, I am immediately rewarded with a certain number of points, and I continue to earn points every time I make a purchase. Moreover, I can accumulate additional points by writing reviews, taking quizzes, and following them on social media, among other things. The process of accessing my points and rewards is also very user-friendly. 13

Primally Pure rewards program is so effective that they are always top of my mind when I need to buy skincare products. Knowing that I can receive better discounts and even free shipping when I buy more only motivates me to purchase more from them. As a loyal customer, I also appreciate that they make me feel valued and appreciated, and this only strengthens my loyalty to their incredible brand. #obsessed

Case Study: Starbucks

Starbucks has one of the best loyalty & rewards programs that I've seen. They make it easy to use their program, giving you great incentives to return to them. Starbucks rewards you with points you can use for future purchases in person or on their Starbucks app. The more you buy, the more reward points you get. You can also access bonus rewards such as free coffee, items, or specials/promotions like double points days. 14

The Starbucks loyalty program stands out for its ability to continually offer new and exciting rewards to its customers. Every week, customers have the opportunity to earn bonus reward points by purchasing a featured item. For instance, the current promotion encourages customers to order a mocha at least five times within a five-day period, and in return, they receive an additional 100 stars. One hundred stars are equivalent to a free coffee or breakfast sandwich, which is a significant reward for loyal customers.

Such enticing rewards can motivate customers to visit Starbucks more frequently and continue to earn additional rewards. The program's ability to keep things fresh and new is a key factor in retaining customers and strengthening their loyalty to the brand. When customers open the Starbucks app on their phones, they can see the latest promotions and be inspired to take advantage of the offers, which only adds to their overall experience with the brand.

Customer Referral Programs

"In a world where consumers are more and more bombarded by ads, brand placement, and branded content, word of mouth is a way for consumers to break through that noise." -Extole 15

While a customer loyalty program gets customers to buy more for themselves, a rewards program gets "new people" to buy from you. A customer referral program rewards and incentives your customers to refer friends, family, or followers to buy from you.

Customers who come in through referral are more likely to purchase and have higher LTV (lifetime value). Here are 6 stats you need to hear.

- When referred by a friend, people are **4X more likely to purchase.** 16

- Referred customers' **LTV(lifetime value) is 16% higher** when compared to non-referred customers. 17

- Ninety-two percent of consumers turn to people they know for referrals above any other source. 18

- You can expect at least **16% more in profits** from referred customers. 19

According to Referral Candy- Referral marketing creates a natural word-of-mouth marketing experience for your brand, ultimately increasing your customer retention rate and your revenue. 20

Here are a few key reasons why having a referral program is essential to you if you want to grow your revenue and customer loyalty without using ads:

1. Diversify your customer acquisition channels beyond ads

Something that all businesses stress over is how to acquire a new customer. When you leverage your existing customers, you are essentially using them to get new people through the doors without a penny of ad spend.

2. It rewards your customers, which makes them want to keep referring people your way

It's such a win-win. When you reward your customers for referring someone, they are happy, incentivized, and will keep promoting you!

How Referral Programs Work

A referral program works by inviting current customers to join your referral program and act like "brand ambassadors" for you. When they join your program, they get a unique code or link to share with their friends, family, or followers. The referral program software tracks the activity of a customer's code or link, and when someone makes a purchase, that person gets rewarded, typically in the form of store credit, cash, or a discount. Here's an example from Primally Pure. 21

REFER A FRIEND

Give $10, Get $10

Give your friends $10 off their first order of $50 or more and get $10 (as a coupon code) for each successful referral.

| FRIEND'S EMAIL ADDRESS | | SEND $10 |

This referral process creates a natural word-of-mouth marketing experience for your brand, ultimately increasing your customer retention rate and revenue.

Create A Customer Referral Program

Choose An Incentive

Some referral programs include an incentive for both the referrer and the customer. I think this approach is the way to go because both parties are getting something instead of just offering a reward for the referrer. If you scroll back to the Primally Pure example, they give $10 to the new customer and a $10 coupon to the person who refers.

Other options for referral rewards:

- Free product or a free month of a subscription box

- Points towards a future purchase (this could be more like a loyalty program)

Whichever you choose, know your customers and what incentivizes them!

Choose An App

Here are a few recommended apps that connect with your Shopify store:

- Smile

- ReferralCandy

- Yotpo

- Refersion

*references 22-25

Launch & Grow Your Program

You want to make it easy for people to sign up for your program. Create a page on your online store where people can learn more about your referral program and sign up. This will typically be a link that they can sign up with, and then it will be connected to some kind of dashboard or page where they can view their referrals and any related commission.

Be sure to invite your past customers as well! You can easily send a few emails alerting them of your new program, the incentives and what it includes, and how they can get started and join. Patchwork Pet, for example, sends an email to existing customers to promote its referral program. 26 Each email contains a unique referral link for its customer to share and a clear explanation of what they (and their friends) will get in return:

patchworkpet

Share the *Patchwork Pet* LOVE

Refer friends. Get rewards.

Give your friends 20% off all products. Get 25% off discount code on your next order when they shop with your link.

Share Invite Link

Continue Promoting The Program

Here are some ways to continue to grow your referral program while automating quite a bit of it.

- **Email Marketing:** *In your post-purchase emails* and *Order Confirmation emails-* This is the perfect opportunity to grab their attention while they are excited about receiving your product.

- **Social Media:** *Leverage "saved responses" in Instagram-* Whenever a happy customer or a customer tags you in an Instagram post, story, or TikTok, take that as your opportunity to invite them to be part of your referral program. You can create a saved response in your DM's, create one quick message that invites them to join, and then be able to send it off in seconds.

For my business, The Dapper Dog Box, this was a Prime way of getting customers to refer all their friends and family my way. Whenever I had a happy customer, I would send them a quick message and tell them how they could win a free product, how they could join, and what the next steps were. It was so easy, and this allowed me to get hundreds and hundreds of customers to refer friends and help my business grow without much effort.

The Scrappy DIY Customer Referral Strategy

My DIY version of this is in case you can't afford an app or don't want to pay for an app. It's also so simple if you get past the manual aspect of it.

Each and anytime you have a happy customer, invite them to be part of your customer referral program. You can say:

"Thanks so much for your support. We value you so much as a customer of our {insert brand}. Did you know you can get (insert incentive), for example, free shipping, cash back, points towards a future purchase, or a free product by referring a friend or family member/follower. Here is what you need. We create a discount code for you, and if anyone uses it, you get the {insert incentive}. Would you like me to create a coupon code for you?

That's it! It's so easy and breezy for you. Simply choose an incentive and get started! The easiest thing is a dollar value per coupon used or a discount % per coupon used. This makes it super easy for you. All you have to do is send them that code each month as it's used. This method is very manual and takes some time, but it works well, especially if your customer base is small.

Case Study: How She Created A Word of Mouth Referral Funnel

Kristin Fisher, Founder & CEO of Bocu (gift box brand) 27

"Unknowingly, I created a business that is built on referrals. My gift box brand, Bocu, began as a one-off occasion gifting business. The beauty of this niche is that each gift box (ie: each transaction) touches two customers. The gift sender and the gift recipient. I quickly saw the opportunity to turn the sender into a loyal repeat customer through the post-purchase experience and a robust rewards program and the recipient into a first time customer through a stand-out unboxing experience. How do we know if we're converting those recipients into customers? Through a tracked QR code inside the box with an irresistible offer encouraging them to send a gift to someone else! This ripple effect resulted in a 60% returning customer rate.

Our #1 goal in 2022 was to get that number to 40% so that we could increase traffic to convert new first-time customers while continuing to nurture our existing loyal customers. (good problem to have, right?)

Our organic growth led to a custom gifting program that scaled the business past six-figures within its first year of launch - driven entirely, 100% by referrals from one custom gifting customer to another. This happened either by word of mouth based on their easy experience working with us and/or the results that they saw once their own clients, employees or attendees received their gifts. Or the referral simply happened after someone received and loved their gift, and wanted to give that same experience to their own clients or employees.

We treat the post-purchase experience for custom gifting just like we do with our ecommerce side of the business - including tailoring a specific box insert to encourage recipients to contact us for their own business. We understand the value of a loyal, repeat customer. Whether it's a single box order or a 1000 box order, we are obsessed with each customer and want them to become obsessed with Bocu! Create an amazing experience and you'll have your customers shouting from the rooftops about your brand."

Next Steps:

Generate More Passive Sales Through Customer Referral & Loyalty Programs

Start a Loyalty or Referral Program

Consider starting a customer loyalty & rewards program- choose the platform, incentive, and start promoting. Hint hint- SMILE app will let you have a loyalty program & referral program all in one platform.

Brainstorm 5 New Ways To get Your Customers To Buy More From You

In addition to loyalty programs and apps, can you brainstorm 5 ways to get your customers to buy more from you?

1. _____

2. _____

3. _____

4. _____

5. _____

Leverage Email Marketing For Loyalty

How can you better leverage email marketing to invite past customers to buy more and invite subscribers on your list to buy for the first time. Make a list of 10 emails you can send to your list over the next few months that could encourage them to buy more.

1. _____

2. _____

3. _____

4. _____

5. _____

6. _____

7. _____

8. _____

9. _____

10. _____

Chapter 8:
Your Time To Create a Cult-Like Brand Starts Today

Throughout this book, you've learned how to create a mega customer-centric brand that obsesses over its customers and ensures they have the most incredible experience. You are on your way to creating a cult-like brand that your customers are obsessed with because now you understand how to create an epic experience for them, how to create customer service systems, how to create a sense of community, involve your customers and lastly- how to retain your customers, so they come back for more, again and again.

I hope I've proven that this is 100% possible for you. But you also know it will take hard work to get there, even with strategy in place. Most entrepreneurs don't have the guts that you do but remember you still need to take action. Nothing happens by reading a book, but small incremental changes can happen once you take action and take control over your business. You DO have the power to create the brand of your dreams- one you are currently obsessed with.

The last thing I want you to consider is this:

What kind of brand do you want to build?

Do you want one that people talk about year after year?

Do you want one that can be built up and sold eventually? (hint hint. I did this, and I highly recommend it)

Do you want a brand where customers gush all over you on social media?

If you answered yes to these questions- this book will help you get there.

Keep this book as a reminder of everything you can do to create your own wildly obsessed customer superfans. Return to the chapters and exercises and implement as many things as possible.

You DO have the power to create the brand of your dreams- one you are completely obsessed with.

A Final Message

This isn't goodbye. I hope we'll see each other at an event or one of my in-person retreats one day.

I am cheering you on, rooting for your success, and I'm here to help you. I pride myself on being a hype girl for so many female entrepreneurs in the world.

If you want to work with me further, remember I am only a click away. You can join my programs and coaching programs, like The Cultish Product or anything else, by visiting *www.kerriefitzgerald.com.*

Cultish Product is my coaching program that teaches you how to create your own cult-like brand. You can can learn more by visiting my website, *https://www.kerriefitzgerald.com/cultish*

Just remember, you can build the business you dream of. You only have to remember these key strategies.

- Your customers are THE lifeline of your business. Do whatever you need to take care of them, and make them feel special and part of your brand.
- Always reward and incentivize your top customers
- Create the customer service systems that you wish you received as a consumer

- It's 5X easier to retain a customer than to get a new one

- Customers who love and feel connected to your brand will tell their friends, family & followers about you- more visibility and eyeballs on your business with zero advertising.

- You have the power to create a cult-like brand

And if you remember nothing else, remember this: Treat your customers like humans, and they will come back. Always strive to create the most customer-centric brand, and you will attract customers who are wildly obsessed with you.

It's your time. Why not your brand?

Xo. Kerrie

P.S. If you liked this book, please share it with your business besties or in business groups. I'd also LOVE to see a picture of yourself reading this book- it honestly makes my whole world. Tag me on Instagram @kerrie.a.fitzgerald

Keep in touch, my beautiful friends, and never stop chasing the dream of creating a customer-obsessed brand.

Instagram: **@kerrie.a.fitzgerald**

Podcast: The 6 Figure Product Business Podcast
{listen on Apple, Google, Spotify}

Youtube : **www.youtube.com/kerriefitzgerald1**

www.kerriefitzgerald.com/podcast

Download your book bonuses here:
www.kerriefitzgerald.com/cobonus

Download Your Free Bonus Gift

THE FREE CUSTOMER OBSESSION BONUS COMPANION COURSE

As a thank you for buying my book, I'm giving you a bonus gift of supplemental information about creating your own customer-obsessed brand, 100% FREE.

Your free gift comes with downloadable worksheets, bonus videos, and resources mentioned in this book but created to help guide you through Customer Obsession.

- 3-Part FREE Customer Obsession Companion Course: Here, I walk you through the key modules from this book, accompanied by videos, cheatsheets, and templates.

- 3-Part Email Sequence Templates: I share my exact email templates to help you nurture your buyers into superfans overnight.

- Additional downloadable worksheets, bonus videos, and resources mentioned in this book.

Visit the following link to download
www.kerriefitzgerald.com/cobonus

References

Chapter 1: What Is Customer Obsession

1. Thomas J. Law, Oberlo, " 19 powerful ecommerce statistics that will guide your strategy in 2023"https://www.oberlo.com/blog/ecommerce-statistics

2. Invesp, https://www.invespcro.com/blog/customer-acquisition-retention/

3. The Barkday Planner, https://www.thebarkdayplanner.com/

Chapter 2: The Importance of Your First 100 Customers For Your Business

1. Noura Blanc www.nourablanc.com

2. The Fragrant Nest www.thefragrantnest.ie

3. Stroud Simply Southern www.stroudsimplysouthernco.com

4. Do Good Adventures www.dogood-adventures.com

Chapter 3: The Importance of Customer Experience

1. The Content Planner https://www.thecontentplanner.com/

2. L'atelier Box https://latelierbox.com/

3. Amazon www.amazon.com

Chapter 4: How to Create an Unforgettable Customer Experience

1. https://kerriefitzgerald.com/magical-ecommerce-packaging

2. Patchwork Pet www.patchworkpet.com

3. Paypal- www.paypal.com

4. Shopify www.shopify.com

5. Stickermule- www.stickermule.com

6. 99designs www.99designs.com

7. EcoEnclose, https://www.ecoenclose.com/

8. Packlane, https://packlane.com/

9. Pratt, https://www.pratt.com/

10. Boxup, https://www.boxup.com/

11. Uprinting, https://www.uprinting.com/

12. Stickermule, https://www.stickermule.com/

13. Lumi, https://www.lumi.com/

14. Vistaprint, www.vistaprint.com

15. Catherine Hildner, Kitty Meow Boutique, https://kittymeowboutique.com/

Chapter 5: Nail Down Your Customer Service

1. Real Dog Box, Cancel Culture, Drama https://www.reddit.com/r/rawpetfood/comments/kesh0t/real_dog_box_cancel_culture_drama/

2. Zendesk, https://www.zendesk.com/

3. Gorgias, https://www.gorgias.com/

4. Help Scout, https://www.helpscout.com/

5. Freshdesk, https://www.freshworks.com/

Chapter 6: Create Community & Get Customers to be involved with your brand

1. Ripley & Rue- www.ripleyandrue.com

2. Allie Ruby, Pseudo Force, https://pseudoforcestudio.com/

3. Emily Mariko, https://www.tiktok.com/@emilymariko

Chapter 7: Customer Retention & Loyalty

1. Pr Newswire, New Retail Study Shows Marketers Under-Leverage Emotional Connection, https://www.prnewswire.com/news-releases/new-retail-study-shows-marketers-under-leverage-emotional-connection-300720049.html

2. Fuego Box- www.fuegobox.com

3. Invesp, https://www.invespcro.com/blog/customer-acquisition-retention/

4. Shopify, Jessica Wynne Lockhart https://www.shopify.com/enterprise/how-ecommerce-brands-can-prepare-for-apples-ios-14-update

5. Shopify Elise Dopson, https://www.shopify.com/enterprise/ecommerce-customer-retention

6. Gorgias, Ryan Baum, https://www.gorgias.com/blog/ecommerce-churn-rate

7. Shopify Elise Dopson, https://www.shopify.com/enterprise/ecommerce-customer-retention

8. Shopify, Ecommerce Customer Retention Marketing: How to Use Emails, Loyalty Programs & Communities to Improve Retention- https://www.shopify.com/enterprise/ecommerce-customer-retention

9. Forbes, Katherine Black, https://www.forbes.com/sites/kpmg/2017/09/13/why-customer-loyalty-programs-are-so-important/?sh=44201df72bd4

10. Smile, https://smile.io/

11. Yotpo app https://www.yotpo.com/integrations/

12. Referral Candy app https://www.referralcandy.com/

13. Starbucks- www.starbucks.com

14. Primally Pure www.primallypure.com

15. Extole 15 referral marketing statistics you need to know, https://www.extole.com/blog/15-referral-marketing-statistics-you-need-to-know/

16. Growsurf 9 compelling marketing statistics you need to know, https://growsurf.com/blog/9-compelling-referral-marketing-statistics-you-need-to-know

17. Knowledge at Wharton, July 21, 2010 https://knowledge.wharton.upenn.edu/article/turning-social-capital-into-economic-capital-straight-talk-about-word-of-mouth-marketing/

18. Forbes Love It Or Hate It: Influencer Marketing Works Daniel Newman

https://www.forbes.com/sites/danielnewman/2015/06/23/
   love-it-or-hate-it-influencer-marketing-works/

19. Harvard Business Review,Philipp Schmitt, Bernd Skiera,Christophe Van
    den Bulte Why Customer Referrals Can Drive Stunning Profits https://hbr.
    org/2011/06/why-customer-referrals-can-drive-stunning-profits

20. Referral Candy https://www.referralcandy.com/blog/47-referral-programs

21. Primally Pure www.primallypure.com

22. Smile, https://smile.io/

23. Referral Candy, https://www.referralcandy.com/

24. Yotpo, https://www.yotpo.com/

25. Refersion, https://www.refersion.com/

26. Patchwork Pet www.patchworkpet.com

27. Kristin Fisher, Bocu, https://www.shopbocu.com/

About The Author

Kerrie Fitzgerald is a serial entrepreneur, e-commerce business coach, mentor, educator, and speaker who has spent the last 7+ years helping countless female entrepreneurs take a business idea and turn it into a brand that customers are obsessed with.

She started her first business, The Dapper Dog Box, and turned it into a best-selling brand, reaching multi 6 figures in sales with zero ads, staff, or funding. Today Kerrie helps savvy action-taking female e-commerce brands and helps them create their customer-obsessed brand.

Kerrie lives outside Seattle with her family & two beloved dogs.

Find her at **www.kerriefitzgerald.com**

Instagram: **@kerrie.a.fitzgerald**

Youtube : **www.youtube.com/kerriefitzgerald1**

Podcast: The 6 Figure Product Business Podcast
{listen on Apple, Google, Spotify}

www.kerriefitzgerald.com/podcast

Download your book bonuses here:
www.kerriefitzgerald.com/cobonus

www.ingramcontent.com/pod-product-compliance
Lightning Source LLC
Chambersburg PA
CBHW071707210326
41597CB00017B/2370